D1560358

A Restored Life

A Restored Life

My Journey To Healing

by

Kyle Walker

JAHbookdesign

Printed in the United States of America

First Edition: Feb 2018

10 9 8 7 6 5 4 3 2 1

ISBN-13: 978-1985887763
ISBN-10: 1985887762

Cover Design by Joshua Holmes

Dedication

This book is dedicated to my Parents. I can't say thanks enough for taking care of me and raising me with the Love of Jesus.

Isaiah 55:10 ESV

"For as the rain and the snow come down from heaven and do not return there but water the earth, making it bring forth and sprout, giving seed to the sower and bread to the eater…"

Contents

Introduction

The writing of this book is not to hurt anyone by leaving them out or to blame anyone. This is just me telling my story of how I lived since identifying the symptoms of what I can only assume is Babiesa Lyme Disease, in simplistic terms. It was undiagnosed, as you will find throughout the book. This is my coming out, from my point of view, what I felt inside and out, in hopes to inspire, create awareness for those that don't quite understand how real the symptoms of unknown diseases from ticks are. I also hope, in reading this book, if you don't know already, that you will know that God uses anyone no matter what he or she faces, living through you to build character and hopefully a relationship with Jesus Christ, like He did me, if only you will give Him a chance to save you and do works in you too.

Part One
Time Of Mystery

PROLOGUE
Love of the Woods

B EFORE THE AGE of 14, I used to love going up into the woods, still do. I used to make pathways going up and through the woods. Started making them with my neighbor Jerry, and on the days he didn't come up I'd finish them.

I started the path up past our wash line, and I wove it up and around where there was room for a rake to go through. The path went up to the fort.

Jerry and I also started using caution tape as the walls. I don't remember the exact dimensions, but it had three or four rooms. On some days the fort became a star ship (I loved Star Trek). Jerry could make the sounds of the Enterprise to a tee, he was that good.

Then I started making paths from the back door of the fort to the field and other side trail paths back, and I enjoyed it. Jerry and I had a blast with our imaginations running our adventures through the woods up until 16 to 18.

Everything just became harder to maintain because my tightness was getting worse in my legs, especially on the bad days. I had to start taking lawn chairs and buckets for me to sit on, had used them for Captain chairs anyway.

Still, the days I'd go up in the woods became less and less because I was getting so tired of my legs tightening on me to the point of feeling like I picked up one of the logs in the woods.

But going up in the woods traveling my trails were some of my favorite moments, days. Yes, it might seem silly to some, but it's how imagination grows, it's how poets are born. Plus it was one of the few places I could be myself without fear of being made fun of. I'm not naming anyone (been so long trying to block bad stuff out), but I had enough people funning me. It's probably one of the other reasons I'm cautious about when and to whom I talk.

It definitely didn't help when I started to stutter. Yes, I've had a few make fun of the way I talked.

My teenage years after 16 weren't always easy. I had my hard days and harder days, probably the days I listened to music the most, dreaming I was at a different place, in a western adventure, traveling on my favorite horse.

If I was reading my favorite western, I was making my own in my mind. In my dreams, I was free of pain and saving people from their pain.

Probably why I love the gift the Lord has given me in poetry, because I hope it helps relieve pain for others. I just didn't want others feeling the pain inside that I felt at times. My pain eased when the emotions of my pain came out on paper and helped others feel better.

As my symptoms worsened, as the years went by, I became lost, and the things I loved doing became harder and harder to do. My weight kept going up, too. The only activity that has kept me from totally losing it is golf. Instead of walking up into the woods making trails, I'd walk up trying to find golf balls that I hit on good days when my legs weren't being a pain.

The only One to keep me from giving up has been Jesus Christ and my Living Dream to be a big impact for His Kingdom.

My dream of being a ball player died a long time ago, my dream of being on the PGA tour (LOL) was more to keep my mind distracted from pain, my dream of having a family of my own giving my Parents grandchildren is hard to come by when I can't go anywhere. But my dream through poetry to finally do something I can be proud of is real, and I can say I accomplished something important despite an inability to go anywhere on my own two feet.

Feeling Cool

CHAPTER ONE
Retracing Steps

HOW DOES A lost, depressed Christian start his story? By retracing his steps until he finds the right path intended to follow Jesus. Not that I was really depressed, but I was admittedly confused when one dream after another started breaking.

I grew up wanting to play baseball, wanting to be an MLB pitcher, until my heart wasn't in it. Then my body started breaking down when I was 14. It happened to be my last year of youth baseball, and I never played on a team after that.

Also, that year was the only time I got flu-like symptoms. All my life, I've lived in the country, by the way, surrounded by woods, and unfortunately found no doctors to take ticks seriously. So I lived with undiagnosed Babiesa Lyme Disease till I turned 36, the summer of 2016.

I was raised by Godly Parents, went to church Sundays and Wednesdays, grew to love Jesus early, plus walked with a best friend, a pastor's son, along with other Godly friends.

Psalm 139:16 are days we're truly known by God our Father before we're born.

I truly was blessed, born in the right place, right time, with a righteous upbringing with Silas's mentoring by apostle

Paul's. But still, the battles of life weren't easy. Just because we're saved early doesn't mean roads are easy to walk. The obstacle course waits for all Warriors, what one becomes when accepting Jesus Christ as Savior.

God uses trials to test our faith. He tested mine at age 16. My lower leg and forearm muscles started contracting called them walking with vice grips tightening on every step taken. I had no clue what was going on, didn't know how to explain it. How can our explanation make sense if we don't know what it is ourselves?

I would be helping with fire wood collection, or helping clear the driveway ditch, and depending what body part I'd be using, more legs or arms would tighten to the point I thought my calves and shins would pop like a balloon. They felt like logs instead of legs. I first tried walking through the pain, and then through the numbness. It was a scary feeling when my feet started falling asleep during the attempt.

So I would often take breaks on jobs, and would get fussed at for not working enough. I know it looked like I was being lazy, just wanting to get out of chores to play video games early. But truth was, I just wanted the physical and mental pain to stop. Life's not easy when you aren't understood or taken seriously. Games just became my ice, a way to keep my dreams alive.

Thankfully, Christian music also started becoming my safe haven, which opened a door for my daydreams to go. Reading Western books by Stephen Bly, Louis L'Amour offered another outlet. Every book would take my mind on the next adventure, far away from the physical, mental pain. Don't ask me for road directions, I don't see road signs in my visions. Louder the Music the better I could focus on my dreams/visions. Little did I know I was training my mind to craft my God-given gift of seeing visions of poetry?

I WAS THANKFUL that God gave me the gift of poetry, even though I never read poetry (since it wasn't a Western book).

My weight gain was overcoming my physical weakness, lack of activity, and medications for chronic pain. I saw doctors for muscle diseases, but the side affect was weight gain.

So here I was with real world dreams dying, physical problems, not to mention stuttering, which also started at 16. And yet I was only taken for shy, because I didn't talk much.

#1 my legs wouldn't take me far to walk up to someone, plus fear of being made fun of for not getting words out fast enough. But again little did I know God was using my time to observe people around me, people watching to help inspire me.

But still, mentally, battles were going on. I hated my picture taken, because, looking back, Truth was I hated the way I looked. I felt lost, broken and confused. I just didn't want my photo taken then, since it showed how fat I had become.

One day I was in a chat room, witnessing my faith in Christ to someone with a hardened heart. I walked away, deep in thought, asking God why it was so difficult to witness.

It just so happened to be a day my legs were working, allowing me to exercise without muscle contractions, and I was listening to music deep in my dream vision state of mind when I heard a voice as clear as if talking to someone face-to-face.

The Great I Am was present. He gave me my first song lyrics/poem to write. He not only revealed I Am, the title of my first poem, but also the Scripture.

Monday, June 10, 2002
I AM

I am the Creator of heaven and earth
I am the Light of the world
I am the One that led Moses to the Promised Land
I am the One that wrote the Ten Commandments
I am the One that tore down the walls of Jericho

Why won't you believe that I am the One for you?
Why won't you believe that I am the One that loves?
Why won't you believe that I am the One that saves?
Why won't you let Me save you today?

I am the Stone that killed Goliath
I am the One that held the lions for Daniel
I am the One in the fiery furnace.
I am the King of kings

Why won't you believe that I am the way?
Why won't you believe that I am love?
Why won't you believe that I am the father?
Why won't you put your faith in Me?

I am the One that came from heaven to earth
I am the One that healed the blind to see
I am the One that healed the sick
I am the One that healed the man of leprosy
I am the One that fed the five thousand

I am the One that raised Lazarus from the grave
I am the One that took your place to die
I am the One that shed blood to save man from sin
I am the One that was raised in three days
I am the One that way to heaven

Why won't you believe I am the Truth?
Why won't you believe I am the Everything for you?
Why won't you believe I am the Savior of the world?
Why won't you believe in Me?

My Uncles are a big part of my life. It was my Uncle Tim that took my cousin Isaac and me to Philadelphia, to tryout for the Phillies with the dream of being a MLB pitcher still alive, two years before throwing into one of those pitching machines at Camden Yards. Pitching 85 mph, with control, was good enough for me to still believe.

Unfortunately, the year after that, my shoulder – which had been giving me fits, like in my forearms and legs – hurt when throwing, and it took me 30 minutes or more to warm up, to loosen enough to throw without pain. Well, one day at my cousin Isaac's baseball practice, I was asked again to throw batting practice. I forgot to warm up like I normally do to avoid the pain, and I definitely felt it on the first pitch thrown. Nevertheless, I kept trying. I'm not one to quit easily.

Weeks later, a doctor told me I had a nerve impingement,

which took the rest of that summer, and all winter to get better. The next summer, I still remember the day July 26th, my once 86 mph came down to 65 mph, which was humiliating, to say the least, seeing my dream flat-lined.

Later that night, however, I wrote my 2nd poem, Voice In The Wind, then after that, my 3rd and 4th. I forget the other titles. But the point is: one dream died, another was being born. I started sharing what I still at the time thought to be song lyrics, but was told wrote good poetry, so I created *Songs Of Poetry*.

One of my biggest fans was my Uncle Mike. I just remember seeing the awe come over his face with a smile in his eyes. Mike loved the Lord. He was also kind enough to help bury my 2nd dog, Duke.

I never got the chance with my 1st dog, Zach, and I blamed myself for the longest time, since letting him out the door when I was eight, I think. Seeing Duke's lifeless body after having him for 13 years wasn't much better, but I still was able to get closure this time.

Dogs and cats, mostly dogs, have been beside me the majority of my life to help me through my hardest times. Though guilt haunts me because of the way I treated them sometimes, which I thought I had gotten from the loss of Zach, I now think my emotional flares are another symptom of Babiesa Lyme disease. Even so, it still doesn't help much.

Anyway, my Uncle Mike helped me, despite health issues. Unfortunately, I lost Uncle Mike to a heart attack the same year I lost Duke. I hoped his helping wasn't the cause.

I hurt like I knew my cousins and my aunt did. He had been so close to me, he was like a second father. But I don't really talk about it. Like most of my mourning period, I fell into deep thoughts, and held my emotions back.

You've got to remember, I never really learned to grieve, so my way was to think of those I loved in a better place with the Lord.

I believed if they were with Jesus, the loved ones were beside Him, just like Scripture says. So when it came to publishing my first book, I had to dedicate it to my biggest fan, Uncle Mike, who finished the Race.

The following poems I wrote after the Phillies tryout, but the last in the series I wrote for my Uncle Mike.

02
Lost in the Storm

Sometimes it feels like life is just going crazy
You just want to find a way out, and start to wander
Where things went wrong and just can't figure it out

Just when it seems like your dreams are at an end
Just when it seems like everything's lost in the storm
The beauty of God is seen and life begins anew (GENESIS 9:13-17)

Sometimes it feels like there's nobody there
When you speak you don't know anybody hears you
Or if anybody cares when feeling down and lost

Just when you feel the storm around you
Just when you thought lightning was going to strike
The Son of God comes in and the storm ends (MATHEW 8:23-27)

Everything will be okay, my child. If you think you're lost in the storm
Just call out my name I'll be there to take your hand
I will calm the storm and lead you to holy ground

02
Voice in the Wind

There is a wind that comes throughout time and space
In this wind there is a voice that can only be heard
A voice that speaks to those that listen

Can we hear the voice in the wind calling us?
Can we recognize the voice in the wind calling?
Saying be still and know I am God

This voice brings those that are lost home
This voice gives strength when we're weak
This voice will heal the hurting
The wind blows wherever it wishes; you hear the sound it makes, but
you do not know

Where it comes from or where it is going. It is like that with everyone
who is born of the Spirit

John 3:8

11/17/04
Legacy

There was a man that served coffee for a living
He was devoted to his family and His church
Then one day the Lord called him home

The King met him in heaven there was a line of people
The King said these are the lives you had an impact on
One says I changed when you said Jesus loved me

We can either live for a legacy here on earth, or in heaven
The legacy on earth will fade, the legacy in heaven will stay
Where we want the greater impact will be up to us

There was a beggar living on the streets he slept in a box
Everyday he read God's word, people would see him pray
Then one day Jesus took him home

The King met him in heaven there was a line of people
The King said these are the lives you had an impact on
One says I changed when I felt you praying

There was a rich man loved money, lived a double life
Gave lots of money to charities, but lived a life of darkness
Never did see past the sin in his life, then demons took him

CHAPTER TWO
Home Alone

S TAYING HOME ALONE most of the time: I did this because my physical problems kept me from driving. But it was still hard to convince people who didn't understand what I was going through.

Yes, some of it was fear of getting behind the wheel, and not knowing when my legs, forearms would tighten to the point of distraction and pain. It wasn't fear for my life, but concern for those I'd crash into.

I just didn't want to cause others pain like mine. So I've been dependent on others driving me. Thankfully, my pets have, for the most part, been around.

It still gets lonely without someone to talk back. The Lord has always blessed me with the perfect companions. When I had Duke, my second dog, I also had two cats.

Mother and Daughter, Fuzzy and Pretty, what can I say about the names? I was young at the time, and kept names simple. I had Fuzzy for 20 years, and I think Pretty for 13 or 14. I didn't handle their passing as well as I would have liked. Since Duke's passing, I struggled, not wanting to have the same memory, seeing him for the last time. Think also why I try to avoid open caskets at funerals.

I know I will see them in heaven again, so I try preserving the good memories. Unfortunately, the bad memories had ways of coming out; especially on the days I snapped and took frustrations out on them. I never really knew why my emotions exploded so, and the guilt was my backdraft punishment.

Fuzzy was the one I attached to most strongly, because she was there for me when Zach, my first dog, left me. The poem I'm about to share was written about her, though it can be read by anyone missing a loved one.

12/26/2006
Memory Of My Love

I don't know why I lost my love after twenty long years
Never to be held close again or the touch of silk to the face
Even though I still feel the painful question of why I know it's ok

I don't know why after twenty strong years then poof after one day
Feelings mixed with pain, sorrow and confusion mixed with gladness
For I know she is in a better place with no pain and with a field of butterflies

I know after twenty long years it was her time to take to the path one last time
Looking back, thinking was there anything else I could have done to preserve
One more day together, but I know it was her time to join the Lord in Heaven

The blame comes even though there's nothing anyone could do against time
But satan will rehash the what ifs to drive guilt in deep like thorns under the nails
Jesus gives me comfort knowing He keeps her safe until I see her

again

Yes I will miss my love of twenty long good years that I have lost of my
life
But I will pick myself off the ground moving on to the life the Good Lord
Has given me, with the memory of my love within of the day will meet
again

CHAPTER THREE
Writing

SOMETIMES I WRITE for people with poem requests, or for those that inspired me.

For the most part, poems I've written have come out of the blue. Well, I hear the Holy Spirit, God speaking to me, through music. Just listening to something when the words stopped going with the song. I am thankful for this.

I've always tried staying humble. It's why I published my first book in 2006 under the pen name Unknown Poet. I didn't want to get caught up in fame, fortune, and lose my humility, or the connection to God that I had.

My whole purpose to keep writing has been about helping people deal with their pain, to make an impact. I originally thought it was impossible to see that I was stuck at home, writing within a small room. But if I could help others heal of their pain, through mine, well what I was going through would be worth it.

Emotions are like roller coasters for me, going up, and then going down, but mostly because of frustration. I got tired of going to doctors and hearing the same thing: counsel to lose weight, that what I was going through was normal.

I never brought up my bathroom issues because I was

losing faith in doctors. Plus, I thought it was too embarrassing to bring up and thought they knew after all that was in my file. I only bring it up now to encourage, because it's not a laughing matter. Those that bring it up are only thinking of their dirty minds. Everyone, everything matters to God our Creator who picked out our every detail on and in our bodies.

Getting bitten by a tick or any other intruder injected into the body: God knows the outcome and the reaction. God could just as easily have used doctors to remove and to heal, but I've been learning He uses these circumstances to move inside, to get close when we're less distracted.

Sometimes getting frustrated and being forced to close doors to be alone, shutting out the outside world is a good thing. This is when we'll know we're not alone, that He's in the closed room with us catching our tears, whispering words of encouragement while hugging our pain away. God truly does give comfort to us even while the Band-Aid gets ripped off.

Keeping me home. God had His purpose for me to interact with people online, playing poker. Those I met online were real people, too, that used poker to get away from problems in the real world. I had published my 1st book with my first 100 poems, working on my second book. While I was playing poker, I was also sharing my poems, meeting new friends, distracting from my pain.

God was using me, and, quite frankly, saving me, showing my purpose at the same time. Donna was one of the friends I met while playing poker and she had a daughter going through troubled times, looking for answers in a bottle.

Given the opportunity, I was able to meet Donielle and talk to her about my faith in Jesus Christ through my poems, which led her to being saved. Which gave me hope that there was something more than me just sitting in my room, feeling I was doing nothing good, that made my life have meaning. I wrote this poem that told our life-changing story.

1/3/2007
Angela

Angela was this woman that was being chased by demons
The demons had her running to the bottle till the last drop
Would wake up the next day without a clue of where or why

Angela's mom would get sick with worry, stricken with fear
Afraid of getting that call to come down to identify her daughter
Then one day she met an Unknown poet and just let it all out

By chance this Unknown poet got to talk with Angela through poetry
Who then started to open up about possibilities of a new hope through Jesus?
Then one day the mom asks the Unknown poet to talk with her

The Unknown poet's heart felt compassion after talking with Angela
Prayed with all His heart and soul that Jesus would cast out the demons
So she could begin the new life through Him

Angela one day decided enough was enough couldn't live that life anymore
Lord she cried out I don't want this life anymore I want something more to life
I give my life to you so you can give a better life to me

A light shines, a fire burns in Angela's soul and walks with Jesus not demons
Instead of running to the bottle she runs to the word of God reading every word
She would make any mother proud with tears that speaks of thanks to the Lord

CHAPTER FOUR
Faith

I LOST MY faith in doctors, even though I still went to them hoping for answers. I was close to losing my faith in getting Social Security Disability (SSDI), in at least having financial help. But, thankfully, my faith in Jesus Christ was strong, and He sent me a lawyer that helped me along. I always held onto my honesty.

I was finally given financial help along with my medical assistance.

I used the back pay to publish my third book, after being disappointed in the way my second book, *Ripples Of Reflections*, was published. Though part of it was because I rushed to publish in time before my Grandfather from my Dad's side passed away from Pancreatic Cancer. But He passed before I was published, and I heard it from the grammar police.

So this time, I wanted my third book, *Rainbows Hidden Treasures*, professionally done. I just had to sell 5,000 copies to get my investment back. I thought if Jesus could feed the 5,000 with two fish and three loaves of bread surely could help me sell 5,000 books.

This was also my first book I worked on with my good

friend, Joshua Holmes. I loved watching him draw in youth group and wanted him to work on my book cover. Unfortunately, the publisher wouldn't let me use it. I should have pulled out then, but the excitement of publishing with someone willing to invest in my book was too good to pass up. It took me a few years to pay back my parents.

Unfortunately, I never sold 5,000. I give away more than I sell. I was given the gift to write Sonnet Poetry, not the gift of marketing or promotion. I couldn't come up with the right words to find interviews for my book, either.

I had a few book signings, but hardly anyone showed up. My legs kept me from walking up to people, my stuttering partly kept me from wanting to talk to people. Mostly though, because my head gets so full of random thoughts, I don't know how to make sense without the headphones on my head providing rhythm of music to separate my thoughts.

My visions don't come to me unless my mind is clear of clutter and of other noises. Maybe that's why I had a hard time passing timed tests, because colored lights, phones ringing distract my concentration. This might be another Babiesa symptom, but God uses me this way.

I've trusted God despite the frustrations. I praise Jesus for being faithful to me. I thank Jesus for being an understanding God who was born through Mary to walk among us. One of the poems I wrote came just looking at a full moon one night, recalling all the moons I saw throughout the years, wondering if the moon was God's eye.

2/21/2008
Eye Of The Moon

Looking up into the eye of the moon can't help but wonder
If it's the eye of the Heavenly Father looking back down at me
And what He is seeing me and what He saw in me to choose me

Seeing the shadows in the light of the eye of the moon can't help
But wonder if that's what He meant even the darkness can't hide
Even in the darkest shadows the eye of the Heavenly Father sees

Still looking up into the eye of the moon can't help but wonder
What did the eye of the moon see way back two thousand years
After all the eye of the moon has been seeing since day one

What was it like to witness your own birth to the world you created?
What was it like seeing your own face kissed by the mother of you?
Was your eye of the moon teary eyed seeing what was to come?

Eye of the moon did you close your eye to the beatings to your flesh
After all the miracles just a few days before you saw yourself give
Now you're seeing them chant crucify to your Holy Name

I know Eye of the moon you saw the future the worth of this sacrifice
Seeing your flesh upon a cross nailed down with a crown of thorn
Are you thinking about all the sins or the day that crown will be of
gold?

For three days Eye of the moon you saw what it would be like without
A living God, I can't help but wonder what that would have been like
But then I shutter looking up in the Eye of the Moon and thank you

Raising up my hands as if waving up at the Eye of the Moon in praise
There's not one word I can say feeling thanks isn't good enough for
coming
I hope giving you my life is enough thanks for coming back Alive

Looking up into the Eye of the Moon can't help but wonder time and
time again
If it's the eye of the Heavenly Father looking back down and what He
sees
But after reading Psalm 139 I know He sees my future in His hands

CHAPTER FIVE
Sports

SPORTS HAS ALWAYS been a part of my life, but I mostly played with friends and family. There was church softball, the only organized team sport I played after little league baseball. This was before my first book was published in 2006, but I was still playing in pain with my right shoulder when throwing, legs tightening after running.

I would have one good burst of hustle down to first or running down a ground ball at second. I just loved competing, the drive to do better, not against, but trying to do better myself. One by one, though, I had to give up playing football in the back yards with family, softball, baseball, too.

I will always be thankful for my Uncle Steve, who got me into golf. Not just to have a sport, but the perfect sport for my physical issues. I could hit my tee shot, then get in the golf cart until my next shot. Plus the competition allowed me a chance to get better. Not just talking about my golf game, but giving me an outlet to relieve frustration, stress without hurting anyone else except a golf ball.

Playing with family has meant more to me than anyone may know. Especially playing in the Timothy Ott golf tournament, which I have never missed, because it's given me the opportunity to make a difference not sitting at a screen plus being able to do something physical, even though it takes me days to recover from the pain afterwards.

At least I was doing something to cause the pain, and not doing anything out of the normal, just from walking in the yard, or just standing in the shower. I'm so humbled having family willing to drive out of the way to pick me up to go golfing.

Truth be told, I don't know what I would have done without being able to golf to get away from the thoughts I get from being around the house alone until my parents come home from work, but still not really having a place to talk it out.

10/1/2009
Little Secrets "in this Poet's Life"

Some days I think I am getting better, other days just don't know
Catch myself staring up at the moon, whether it's there or not in wonder
Will my legs ever be normal again or will they always feel like logs?

I know on the outside I look normal for the most part except under tall
And maybe wider than I should be, it's a big struggle to accept myself

But I keep going on no matter how much pain cause I know time's coming

Hearing about my struggles and body's mysteries feeling how tight I am
Looking back into your eyes, seeing the questions forming to the lips
With all the pain, how do I write the way I do, have to get mad sometimes

Don't get me wrong just like the pain I try to hold the emotions inside me
But then like a volcano I can feel my own lava begin to boil the ash rising
Just when I think my anger, my frustrations overflow, I feel the arms of Jesus

So now you know a little more about this author, this poet's life and little secrets
I know it can be hard to understand and I may never find the answer that I seek
But the one thing that will never change I will never be ashamed of Jesus Christ

How can this be? Strangers will ask and maybe even some brothers and sisters
If you could only hear the way He talks with me out of the blue in odd places
This is how, this is why I write the way I do just love hearing His voice in music

If I could live this life again I wouldn't change a thing not even the pain
Not just because of the people I met turned into dear friends in the Lord
Because deep down I know there's a deeper purpose that only Jesus can see

So until the Lord's plan is complete in me will continue to live the way I do
Because I am not ashamed of Jesus, will always write to live for Him in faith
And maybe one day will be finding answers to my questions

Feeling Isolated to the Changes

CHAPTER SIX
Johnstown

THE YEAR I graduated from homeschool, 1999, and still I hadn't figured out what to do with my life, let alone figured out what I could actually do.

I tried working nights at Ski Roundtop with my Uncle Tim who makes snow, but my job was to clean the tables in the eating area with two weird dudes, I can't remember their names, but for whatever reason they called me Swirl. I had no clue why.

I tried working there for two nights, during which time my left knee really started hurting, which had been bothering me for several weeks, plus the dudes were testing my nerves, not to mention the rest of my lower legs tightening on me because of this I worked as fast as I could, and often didn't have much to do, which was fine.

I'd just watch out the window watching the snowmaking. After two nights, I had enough pain, especially when the big furnace came on, causing my left knee to really hurt, that caused me to quit. But I will never forget the friend I did make, Jana, who's now in Heaven.

It wasn't too long after working at Ski Roundtop I decided to go to some kind of school that evaluated your working skills, and it was my first time being away from home.

The plan was to last two weeks. But double cemented floors soon pained my left knee, my primary care physician (PCP) at the time, whose accent I had a hard time understanding, said I had Athritist.

By the way, I also had a weird roommate, lol. For whatever reason, they kept turning up in my public adventures. Also, I had a fire drill in the middle of the night.

It turned out the test to begin at this school was timed, the kind I struggled with (as I am a visual learner), and the results showed. I was in pain enough, disappointed enough to just walk out the classroom anyway. I didn't want to take any more timed tests, which in my mind didn't reveal the truth of what I could do, especially when given the time.

Most of the time, the only week I was there, I was in physical therapy, for by now both of my knees were killing me with pain. I was having a hard time walking without the lower legs even being involved. I was just plain miserable being at Johnstown. Don't really know why my knees started hurting so bad. The physician working on me at Johnstown disagreed with my doctor's findings.

I guess it could have been a Babiesa Lyme Disease symptom flaring up. But I've never really had the knee pain since. Only God knows for sure what He was using then to guide my path towards who I am today.

CHAPTER SEVEN
Creation Festival

I LOVED GOING to the Creation festival in the '90s, especially from '91 to '93 when I got to hear my favorite bands, Guardian, Bride, and One Bad Pig. The music was on the heavy side, but so were the lyrics deep in faith of Jesus Christ.

I had a significant moment when the drummer of Guardian, Karl Ney, sat under our tarp for the first time, I think in '92, and started talking to me, of all people. I thought it was so cool.

Every year Guardian was there, I would watch for my friend from Guardian, who would actually remember my name. At the few concerts of Guardian outside of Creation that I saw, I made a point to see Karl, who remembered me every time. Karl probably has no idea the impact that he had on my life.

But going to Creation was getting harder and harder as the rest of the 90s grew shorter because of my legs. My family volunteered helping to set up the festival, but I felt so much out of the way and some of the comments I'd get didn't help much either because they didn't understand me. But we had a long stretch from campsite to the Lunatic posse canopy at the top of the hill in the main arena. By the time I made it to the top, my legs felt like they would burst. They'd grow so tight, I couldn't wait to sit.

At the Creation festival in '99, I made a big decision of sponsoring a child from Compassion International because I was actually able to make money that summer, and I felt God calling me to do so. Little did I know the money would end, but thankfully Mom and Dad helped me out, because keeping my commitment meant a lot to me. Breaking away from my principles is not something I want to do.

But after Duke passed and I got Lazz, I finally had to stop going to Creation because the pain in my legs got to be too much, plus my dogs after Duke got too homesick to be alone, even if someone stopped by to feed them, they wouldn't eat so I just stayed home.

Some years were good, other years not so good, as I'd give into really bad eating habits that I'm still recovering from.

I'm hoping to one day go back to the Creation festival if still around when Bosley is cured from separation anxiety, who howls almost the whole time I am gone, even if Mom is still home, though I think he does better every year.

The point of this story is to share that we never know when little moments will turn into big outcomes in our lives. We just never know how big the turn in life really is until we slow down to enjoy the moments of growing into the character that God wants us to be.

CHAPTER EIGHT
Potter County

ONE OF MY favorite places to go was the mountains in Potter County. It was like a second home to me in Pennsylvania. Unfortunately, I didn't go enough. Even though my legs made it hard to walk the mountain trails, I was at peace. I loved watching for deer, and when in the car the occasional black bear. One of the things I loved doing was going spotting at night. Whichever car ride I was on, day or night, I was constantly looking out the window, looking at the mountains and into the valley watching out for wildlife.

We had a cabin in Berg Run, until the unfortunate day we had to sell because the land we rented on had sold. It was one of the saddest days in my life. One of my dreams was to buy my own place in Potter County and live in God's country, as the sign said. I hoped this as we drove past it, and preferably not for the last time.

I've been back about three or four times, but on the North side of Potter, where my Grandparents shared a cabin. I was always so thankful when they invited me along. North Potter was nice, but not the Potter I was used to. The mountains were still breathtaking, but it still took some getting used to new landmarks.

Looking back, though, some of my favorite memories were of the times spent with Grandma and Grandpa and my cousins. I'd share more of the details if I could remember more, like I wish I did.

I've only had one good deer hunting experience when I went with my best friend, his Dad, and brother. We went to a cabin, not to their friend's cabin, but not too far from my Grandparents cabin. It was the only time I had hog-maw and I can't remember what I thought of it.

Going hunting wasn't easy for me because of my legs hurting so basically when we all went our separate ways, I'd walk as far as I could, then find a good spot, looking down the mountainside. Every once in a while, I'd move to another spot. Might have spotted a few doe (was only buck hunting then) it wasn't right to me hunting doe anyway. Because in my thinking, if we killed the mother deer, who would give birth to the buck?

I wasn't really caring about the hunting part anyway. I just enjoyed being in the mountains, spending time with God in my thoughts while watching, waiting for time to pass by. I was on the last hunting day when I got my only action, when I heard a shot on the other side of the ravine and a deer ran down, but I couldn't tell if it was a buck or a doe, and I wasn't going to shoot unless sure. Everything happened so fast. The deer was gone. Looking back, I don't think I had the heart to shoot anyway.

Going home, we went through South Potter and I'm so

glad we did, because we spotted three elks. It was the first time I knew they were in Potter.

The only other time I was back in Potter County was when we took the camper to Sinnemahoning campground with my cousins and my uncle. It was still fun even though visiting the old cabin wasn't the same, literally, as it was totally changed and of course my legs kept me from walking far.

Somehow, my leg contractions always got in the way, but, thankfully, they wouldn't stop my mind from traveling to my favorite mountains.

Potter County was the place my mind would take me most when feeling down or sad. In my mind, when troubles came my way, I'd saddle up my horse in my mind to travel to the sanctuary that would always give me peace.

Hopefully, I will soon go back to the real place I loved in the mountains.

CHAPTER NINE
Dogs

THE LAST TWO pets I've had God knew just what to send me, sensitive dogs. First, there was Lazz – short for Lazarus, and named after the best friend of Jesus. I met Lazz, a Black Lab Collie mix, when he was five weeks old, on Christmas Eve and a few months after Duke passed away. He replaced my late canine's haunting image.

Lazz helped calm me down when I had sudden mood swings, or became frustrated, because he was sensitive to the outbursts and I hated his looks of concern. I'd try to calm down faster. Lazz would also do things that caused me to laugh.

Lazz did hate thunderstorms and would hide in the bathtub. Even when it didn't storm, he would follow Mom or me into the bathroom. He was another loyal friend that God sent me to help me cope with what I was going through.

Growing up, Lazz loved to be outside with me, especially when playing ball. I hit golf balls until we found out Lazz swallowed two of them. I tried to figure out for months why Lazz was frequently throwing up, sometimes for weeks, until one day Lazz was so weak we had to take him to the vet.

Thankfully, my Grandparents on Mom's side actually

drove their Jeep instead of using it for storage with their latest auction buys. But on that day, Lazz lived up to his name. At least one of us became famous. As far as I know, the two golf balls are still there with the story told. Lazz's sickness and the book of Proverbs both helped me write the following poem.

Dog Returns

Watch for Dog drool at the mouth that's the sign it's coming
The fellow brother gets a sick look while holding his stomach
The upchuck is coming, don't let the hurl bring you down

As a dog returns to his vomit, so we will return to our past
Brother, break him gently don't let him carry the burden alone
Go before him clean up his vomit, before it brings him down

Sometimes we don't know we're sick until we get that feeling
We don't know if it's love or the flu, until we feel the flow come
Don't keep it in, let it out test the One that loves you

If he or she can't stand to see you on your knees before the toilet
Then their love isn't worth it if they can't stay with you when you're down
If you're not hurling for the right reasons, then maybe it's you who goes

Thought I'd also share the poem Duke inspired me to write while thinking about His search of a place to ease my burden to see Him pass on.

04/27/05
Trails End

Do we just search for the trails end for a final resting place?
Do we just head for the trails end of no hope, no tomorrow?
Do we just give up when we feel we can't go anymore?

Do we just let nature take its course, walk on the trails end?
Do we just keep walking until we fall, where we drop is the last stop?
The vultures will be the grave marker

The trails end is where we go to take the burden for those we love
The times together were fun but the trails end is calling us home
Where we go only the Creator knows

Snap out of it, we're made in the image of God, not hairy apes
We're children of God we're higher, worth more than the sparrow
We don't search for the trails end

They tried marking the trails end with Christ dying on the cross
Three days later the trails end became the trails start of forever
There is no giving up until Jesus takes us Home in Heaven

After the golf ball episode, Lazz and I stuck to tennis balls and footballs. How I love watching dogs run, having a good time, just the way God intended.

No matter what we go through in life, God knows what it will take to get us through. We just need to trust Him to be faithful to His promise to be with us always.

For nine years, I had Lazz until Lyme disease took him to be with Jesus.

Yes, I believe our pets will be in heaven after helping to take care of us, teaching us God's Love stays with us no matter what we do, good or bad. God's Love will find us and will teach us too, how to love back. I wrote a poem in honor of the fallen, but never have forgotten the furry angels.

No Goodbyes (about my dogs)

The first time left me blaming myself for opening up the door
Before I knew it a rage of anger had built up inside that lashed

At every little failure, just could never get the last image out

Yes life got better, good friends help getting closer to Christ
Heals deep down in the soul, even though the pain of loss
It's never gone away, and the fear of the beast within remains

Second time left me with a burning image of death in nightmares
Because once again never got the chance of saying goodbye
Couldn't wait one more second without getting another Friend

Yes life got better, for ten long years had the cutest puppy face
Though got too big to hold, the lifetime of memories was enough
The beast within was kept at bay; the no goodbyes left my mind

The last time got to do it right, even got to hold him one last time
But I know it won't be for the last time, and he's playing ball
Hurt of loss is there, but with all good memories, the hurt is less

Yes I know this will come across as a sad poem, but when we do it right
Even though it hurts, joy of knowing will still be there, with the healing begun
And the Lord will send another furry friend to be there when we need him

We don't know why God made their lifetimes so short
Just that they're given to us making life just a little easier
But each one will teach us of God's unconditional Love

My current dog is Bosley: half German Shepherd, half Red-haired Hound mix. I found Bosley on Craig's list for a dollar. I wanted to find another dog with personality and I found one with two, I think with two different kinds of barks.

Bosley has the German bark greeting for strangers, and the howl of a hound dog, the friendly response he uses. Bosley also sees himself as the neighborhood watchdog, and definitely watches over me. I am his world, and don't know what I'd do without man's best friend. You could say we needed each other and we're both still a work in progress, still working out our own issues.

We both feel we're not always understood, except when with each other. Bosley did help me make a book (*God's Love and a Belly Rub*). Bosley loves exploring, hunting like a hound was created for, loves chasing squirrels. And I play ball with him when he gets in the mood. I wouldn't be surprised if he has a dog form of ADD.

The only thing you have to know when you come for a visit is to remain calm during the loud greeting until Bosley gets to know you. If you get howled at, it means he likes you, as it's his way of talking to you.

Zach

Duke

Fuzzy and Pretty

Lazz

Bosley

CHAPTER TEN
Private

I'VE KEPT MY struggles private because, compared to others, I felt they were small. But I've been learning each struggle can be bigger when fighting alone, no matter how small. We fall easily to the blindness of the world's ways, reputations, popularity, and success. When we try to measure up to what the world says is good and compare it to what God says, we'll fall short until we surrender all to Jesus. Let Him use the story of our struggles to give others hope, hope that Jesus will save them too.

This is why I'm using the courage to share my stories, to let others that struggle with anything know they're not alone. God will send someone that will help deal with the burden of whatever we carry. Whether it be brothers or sisters in the Lord, or furry friends, or both.

One of my biggest struggles has been my weight issue, over 315 lbs. with type 2 diabetes, which has led to other issues. Sure I could blame Babiesa for my weight gains, but not for emotional eating, stress eating, and out of control binge eating. I've struggled trying to find the triggers so I could stop before getting out of control.

Thankfully, God sent me a Beachbody coach who

happened to live just around the block from me. I met Dawn through my cousin Jessica on Facebook, who posted about Dawn's lost dogs. I think it was God's way to provide me help after hearing prayer after prayer to help me lose weight. I've thought about nothing except trying anything, even though I physically couldn't do much.

Dawn led me to try the 21-Day Fix, 3-day refresh, and 21-Day Ultimate Reset with fitness programs. I did well enough to give coaching a try for the discount at first, and after losing 30 lbs. I tried selling to others. I learned a lot about eating clean from hidden sugars, artificial foods, and portion control. More importantly, I increased the confidence in myself.

After drinking shakes, learning to eat right, I even managed to lower my A1C to 5.7. Within six months, I lost 47 lbs.

One early morning in mid-August, my legs felt so great that I talked myself into walking the three and a half miles to the local grocery store. The temperature was just right for my legs, which struggled in humidity.

Somewhere on the way home, I hurt my back. I completely exhausted my body for days. It took me months to heal my back with extensive physical therapy. I did get to share my books *After God's Own Heart* and *God's Love and a Belly Rub*. So, even when in pain, God uses us to reach people.

I did start backsliding in my weight, however, and I was gaining back what I had worked so hard to lose. I was getting really frustrated, trying everything from starting at the beginning when I first started working with coach Dawn. But nothing really worked, not even the 21-Day Ultimate Reset. I had lost my good focus, my confidence.

Then I lost my Grandfather, who I was very close to. After all, I talked to him all the time, coming in from cutting grass, for numerous seasons ever since I first started mowing for my Grandparents.

For whatever reason, I took losing my Grandma fairly well, then again I've never really cried at funerals. I always stayed strong, knowing they were better off in heaven, face-to-face with Jesus. But, again, I think it also goes with never really understanding how to grieve, so I kept everything inside.

Losing my Grandfather six years after my Grandma hit me harder than I thought it would. I tried talking to my coach, other coaches on the team, but I couldn't really find anyone to talk to that would help take my mind off my grief.

With all the focus on weight loss and health coaching, I had written very little poetry. Yes, I could have blamed those that didn't want to talk with me, was angry enough.

But I believe God was using my grief to get me back to what I was called to do, which is to write poetry for His Ministry. When September came around, I had published my 6th book, *Midnight Ride Of The Son*.

Him Generously (touching many)

My Grandfather is a kind and gentle soul full of humility
I could shake my fist in anger at what cancer is doing
But I choose to take this time with Him great joy

Don't let fear of death, fear of loss on this world steal from us
They have run the race, fought the good fight for the King of Kings
Their just reward is in sight in the very arms of The great I Am

My Grandfather's wisdom will live in the hearts He's touched
Could turn away in anger at what cancer has taken from me
But I choose to take this time with Him Generously

Don't let selfishness steal from those we love blind of their joy
They have passed through a strange world since birth on a mission
They have family, loved ones waiting for them to come home

My Grandfather's endless same jokes will always be remembered
Not because of being told over and over, but because of the joy
Why I can't be angry when death is just a welcome mat to heaven

No need to fear what has no power over us, long as we're His
Not when Jesus will come like a thief in the Night to raise us up
When old, decayed bodies will become new bodies with no pain

Don't stop running the race just because they finished before us
If we'd look around we'll see them now cheering us on every step
They're just no longer alone or in pain, just loving us with Jesus Christ

Shadow Of Me

Born with tight joints and ligaments maybe was start
But still thought had my whole life of dreams ahead
With accepting Christ early in life had my hopes until
Shadows aren't always our own, we just don't see
Not when looking down all the time, need to look up
Even when cloudy, His shadow is there

Since I was 16, felt like a shadow of myself
When my legs would tighten from walking

And no one would understand me

Everyone would ask why am I sitting down instead of working
Push through it and would get better they would say, but didn't
Year after year, got worse instead of better, dreams were dying

Shadows aren't always our own, just hard to tell
When we're always looking down, can't see above
Even in darkest of nights, His shadow is there

All I had going was my faith in Christ, but sometimes not enough
Wanted to play baseball, but couldn't, couldn't stay on my legs
Couldn't stay active enough to keep the weight off

Everyone wondered why I played video games, watched TV
While I was wondering, praying, my body would get normal
All I could do was play my dreams on a screen

Can't drive with legs and arms like these, I thought
But how could I get anybody to understand or get me
When I couldn't understand myself why

Shadows aren't always our own that we see
Self-doubt blinds us to the point of not looking
Not every shadow needs to be feared

Everything started to change day I started hearing His voice
That's when my poetry took hold, started making a difference
Found my calling in mere words, gave hope to others

Shadows aren't always our own, so don't fear
Like the footprints we see aren't always our own
Sometimes He carries us when we can't walk

I may never understand why I was born this way
Some may never get to walk in my shoes to know
But that's okay, I will press on with my shadow

Under the shadow of His wings, will press on
His works through every question in our lives
Will leave us without question, His joy and love

CHAPTER ELEVEN
Tested

URING THE SUMMER, in July and before publishing *Midnight Ride Of The Son,* my Uncle Tim and his bride-to-be got married. I hated having to leave my dog Bosley, didn't really understand why they decided to get married in North Carolina, Sunset Beach, but that's because I didn't know God's plans for me, to finally reveal answers to my prayers; Prayers concerning ailments I'd endured since I was 14 years old.

With my Uncle Steve, Aunt Peggy, and Sister Amy, I stopped at my cousin's house in Virginia Beach. My cousin happened to be a Microbiologist and Lyme disease expert. For a long time, she wanted to test me for Lyme disease, but the distance between us made it hard to do.

Well, I got tested, was able to study my blood with her, and saw the Babiesa parasites. For the next three days I had mixed emotions.

Part of me was glad to finally get the diagnosis. I suspected something like it, but was never taken seriously enough except for my weight issues. I also was feeling anger rise towards the doctors that missed it back in Pennsylvania, one of the leading states in Lyme diseases.

Only my cousin had helped me in diagnosing and in herbal treatments, which I've done for a year. I will always be thankful to my cousin, and my one friend online who was also dealing with Lyme disease and gave my other herbal treatment ideas.

Every doctor I've seen since observing the blood test with my cousin has been one frustration after another. None have taken my cousin's finding seriously. Because I knew what I saw with my own eyes and refused to believe the doctors' ignorance of Tick diseases, I stuck with my cousin's treatments while playing the doctors' treat the symptom game.

After awhile, though, I came to realize that God had His reasons for allowing me physical problems. Questions like, Would I still have been writing poetry with a normal body? Without the pain, would I have been too distracted to write poetry? Would the people, like my friend Donielle, have been helped to get back on the straight and narrow?

My answer was no. Giving up my physical pain, problems wouldn't have been worth the cost. The journey the Lord has taken me through to build my character is for me to write Christian Sonnet Poetry, to help those I meet online, like the Donielles of the world. I may never see the boost of sales with my books, may never know the impact on anyone but Donielle. But that's okay because it's not about the money, never was, never will be. My dream has been to make an impact, to make a difference despite the feeling of going nowhere.

Since leading Donielle to Christ she has been raising two wonderful daughters reading my books of poetry every night. Hearing stories like this is reward enough for me. The money I've spent on publishing my books are worth every penny.

My Life With Undiagnosed Lyme Disease

Life was going so good, could run and play, explore in the woods
Until all that changed, don't know how or when just don't remember
My body just started to change with pain to my feet

Loved playing baseball, football with family until I couldn't run
Just couldn't stand, walk like I used to, feet would hurt to much
Saw a foot doctor but did little good for someone full of life

One day started walking when lower legs started tightening
As if stepped into vice grips that turned tighter with each step
Tried explaining best I could, but just sounded like complaints

Biggest pain from undiagnosed Lyme disease isn't physical pain
But the emotional scaring pain of not being believed for so long
What a relief it was to be taken seriously in my shoes

I know everyone hurts, but my pain was more than physical
Only my Dogs, my friend's that are always there when I needed
Them and the music I listened to gave me places to go in my head

One by one dreams started dying, couldn't pitch in baseball
Shoulders started to hurt, couldn't run, weight was gaining
Other joints were hurting, but was told it was arthritis or tendinitis

Biggest pain from undiagnosed Lyme disease isn't physical pain
But Labeled pains, even though trying my hardest to be pleasing
Couldn't do a single chore without needing breaks every 10 minutes

I know everyone hurts and shouldn't complain about my pain
But it wasn't me trying to be lazy, just couldn't do anything long
So I read to dream, listened to music, to dream just getting away

I thank God for the gift of vision inside my head, giving me places to go
Just to get away from the pain outside and in needed a place of peace
Little did I know would develop my other gift for writing

Part Two

Time Of Reflection

Me Writing Poetry

CHAPTER TWELVE
Self Discovery

THIS BOOK I am writing isn't just another diet book even though it contains tips. I am not trying to diagnose or treat anyone. What I am sharing between these pages are the discoveries that have helped me, and the conclusions I've made. I am simply sharing my thoughts and opinions while thinking back about the journey I've been on to finally come so far.

When I look back, it's hard for me to remember the first steps to the halfway point, because I've tried so hard to forget the painful memories. But in order to share my stories I've had to dig them back up. Yes, you will feel some anger, strong feelings in some of my thoughts and opinions, but then the anger will subside when the Truth reveals the hidden purpose behind the brokenness, behind each painful step.

The Truth is that we need to go on these journeys of self-discovery to learn what we're made of, and what details God our Creator put inside of us. I encourage you to read about the making of the Tabernacle (Exodus 25), even though the reading gets to be tedious, especially the readings about every single detail that went into the making of the Tabernacle, starting with the Ark of the Covenant.

The point is: This same kind of detail went into making each one of us. We're all made to be different to serve in different ways, through the difference God uses in building our character. Showing how we're adapting through the hard times in our Journey of self-discovery is how we inspire others to build confidence, build courage to keep trying new things while leaning on faith, learning to trust Jesus to be there, to catch them when they too fall.

Making mistakes, stubbing toes in the dark is the way we learn to slow down, and not to go faster than Jesus Christ, who's leading us. Yes, we need to watch where we step, but not to the point of not looking up and not seeing where Jesus turns in different directions. Looking up keeps our view pointed toward the Light Who is our Path.

Psalms 119:105 "Your word is a lamp to my feet and a light to my path." Let the Word of God direct you in the journey of self-discovery. Find out what helps in growth, and what weakens, what holds you back. Will find we're already born broken, and the Journey of self-discovery is how we find the path toward healing.

There's no reason to fear being broken when we already are. We're already walking dead. We're born sinners, so the only fear we have is letting Jesus put us back together again, and the fear of being Born again, leaving the familiar darkness we've always known.

The journey of self-discovery will reveal the empty space in our hearts, which will lead to hearing the knocking at the door until Jesus is let in.

But the journey doesn't end there, because Jesus wants to take you on more journeys of discovering what the dreams mean, discovering your purpose is so much more than serving in our own little world.

You will discover it is possible to serve while still broken, that the comfort in living broken comes from giving thanks in praise to the Lord even when Satan lays bets to the world you will fall apart in cursing God instead of praising Him.

Reverting back to our old selves, it will be the blinders that keep us from seeing the progress Jesus is making in our healing. Learning to walk in patience, while learning to walk in our prayers.

James 1:6-8 "But let him ask in faith, with no doubting, for the one who doubts is like a wave of the sea that is driven and tossed by the wind. For that person must not suppose that he will receive anything from the Lord; he is a double-minded man, unstable in all his ways."

In other words, learning to walk in confidence. Learning about the fruits of the Holy Spirit, as well as the foods good for the flesh that nourish, and learning what grieves the Holy Spirit when we get into other spirits that are not of God. And I'm not just talking about alcohol, but food addictions, all addictions of lust, gluttony.

I've had to learn these things. We all need to learn in our differences, while at the same time learning to accept help from those that have already gone before us and have come back to help us finish what God started in us.

We don't have to understand how something works in

order to use it. We don't all understand how a cell phone is made, but we still use it without that understanding. We don't all understand how a car is made to work, but we still drive one. If we can place faith in things we use yet don't understand to keep them working for us in our time of need, then why can't we place faith in the Living Word of God even though we don't truly understand, and still trust Him enough to keep working in us, through us, provide for us, even when those of logic tell us not to?

From those that don't even want us to understand, through their science that proves nothing because they refuse to believe, because they still have yet to take their journey of self-discovery.

The first step begins with trusting there is something more to trying to understand before taking the initiative. Second step involves faith, believing full understanding isn't needed in order to follow where the questions lead to the answer, no matter the direction or storms that we have to go through. Learning to walk in fear while combining the first two steps, is step three.

Matthew 14:26-32 "But when the disciples saw him walking on the sea, they were terrified, and said, "It is a ghost!" and they cried out in fear. But immediately Jesus spoke to them, saying, "Take heart; it is I. Do not be afraid." And Peter answered him, "Lord, if it is you, command me to come to you on the water."

He said, "Come." So Peter got out of the boat and walked on the water and came to Jesus. Jesus immediately reached out his hand and took hold of him, saying to him, "O you of little faith, why did you doubt?" The fourth step is repeating the first three over and over until total surrender to what Jesus has in store for the journey of accepting Jesus is the Answer we seek and building the relationship of Trust through Faith is the key to finding any healing without losing any hope in getting through.

Will know when you made it, when God's timing and your desires meet, then you will know the understanding that you needed to start was with you all along. The understanding found, is that will meet people, pets in your life that will walk with you on your journey until it's time to take the turn that will bring new people in your life.

Don't lose heart when they walk away or feel they're turning against you, because it's not about you and them anymore. They've served their purpose in building your character. Now it's time for others with different skills needed to take your character to the next level God wants you to be.

Reading the book of James over and over until lived will help against the doubts that will try holding you back. Satan will try putting bitterness in your heart instead of the pure Joy going through these tests of strengthening Faith.

Jesus is just waiting for us to break away from the fear holding us back, to trust in His voice to call for us to get out of the boat and use our little faith to take a walk out on the waters of life with Him. Do this obediently, and He will provide you with the miracles that you seek like He did for me.

*   *   *

GOING THROUGH THE most painful years of my life was hard: from not being understood, or able to put into words what my body felt like when acting up for people, especially doctors, so they would listen.

But now going back through these painful memories to write this book, I can see the value of the pain that I was going through. The value of pain is hard to see living in the past, when trying everything to escape the feel of pain. Once the grip has gotten hold, you feel the grip getting tighter and tighter. Except escape isn't possible when we can't relax enough from past circumstances to let go.

Sticks and stones may leave scars from healed bruises, but words, even misspoken words in time of frustration, anger leave long lasting bruises from within that no Band-Aid can fix. I know it feels that we're alone with nobody in sight when dealing with pain that won't let go, and not talking about physical pain, but mental, spiritual pain.

The Truth is, we're never alone. Jesus is there with us, and, believe me when I say it, He neither wants us to have the pain we go through, nor wants us to see something that isn't meant to be.

Instead, He wants us to let go the pain and see the painted picture that the pain represents. The Apostle Paul spoke of a thorn in his side.

2 Corinthians 12:7-10 "So to keep me from becoming conceited because of the surpassing greatness of the

revelations, a thorn was given me in the flesh, a messenger of Satan to harass me, to keep me from becoming conceited. Three times I pleaded with the Lord about this, that it should leave me. But he said to me, "My grace is sufficient for you, for my power is made perfect in weakness." Therefore I will boast all the more gladly of my weaknesses, so that the power of Christ may rest upon me. For the sake of Christ, then, I am content with weaknesses, insults, hardships, persecutions, and calamities. For when I am weak, then I am strong."

I am also reminded of a Jason Gray song "the wound is where the light gets in," which is so true especially in this day and age with every distraction available to keep us from spending time with the Lord. Without the pain we get would we remember to let the Lord in to spend time with Him, so someone, something else doesn't take His place? We will either have the grip of Jesus holding us, or that of satan. Don't know about you, but I know I chose the one with the firm, maybe a little rough where the nail went through, but His grip gives comfort. Where satan's grip is slimy so we keep falling into his thorns.

The value of pain is hard to see let alone measure the worth of having in our life. But if we view pain as another window opening for Jesus to get through, then let it be a reminder to keep the door open next time Jesus wants to spend time with you.

It's hard to build up enough courage to walk where pain waits, either in plain sight or hidden in the bushes of reality. But if you see that it's not pain holding us back, you'll also see its fear.

Take, for instance, the Bible story of Jesus walking on water in the storm calling Peter out of the boat to join Him. But what we don't read is about what the other 11 disciples did, like after seeing Peter, did they get the courage to walk out onto the water? Or did they let fear keep them inside the boat, the fear of the pain from drowning?

But it was Peter that we read used the courage faith in Christ gives to find the value of pain, which is seeing what Jesus can do when we keep our eyes on Him and not on what is happening to our flesh, our feelings of emotions.

Again, I go back to the point of already being broken and most of the pain we go through is from healing. The only way to tell and see the difference between pain received as if walking into a bush of thorns, or as healing pain as the thorns are being taken out of the flesh and the wounds are being cleaned. The only way to tell is to let Jesus take the thorns out of our bodies, physically, mentally and spiritually. The value will be found when we see the Truth of Jesus bandaging our brokenness, putting the pieces back in place until mended.

Getting healthy is more then about what we eat or drink past our mouths. Getting healthy is also about dealing with what's between the ears. Yes, the adrenals play a part in stress, but it's also a scepter of mental and emotional stress. Which goes with the pain and brokenness I've been opening up and talking about. This is also why we need Jesus Christ accepted in our hearts as Savior, not just as life insurance. But it is a relationship with Him that gives us a relationship to the Father, to the connection to comfort and peace that only Jesus gives living inside of us.

Without Jesus our soul is feeling empty, always on fight or flight in desperation to find something, someone to fill that empty void in our lives. Until we accept the Truth of Jesus being the only One that will satisfy that void, we will keep stressing.

Even though I was still having health issues nobody could solve, it was my faith in Jesus Christ that kept me going, even getting through the pain. Looking back I can now see the value of the pain that I felt, not seeing when I first felt pain doesn't matter, what does matter even when asking the Why is that I kept going and still keep going as Jesus leads the way to healing. Sometimes healing means helping others, resting from your needs and helping others with their needs. Sometimes we're the wounded being bandaged, other times we're the bandage going around the wound and stopping the bleeding of someone else. This is how they get to see the value of pain, when they see, feel the hands of Jesus working on them.

Then they will know the pain they're going through is from healing and they can let go the bitterness that keeps them from feeling well and letting the healing begin.

Getting the mind, Spirit, and body healing as one, will be the icing on the cake, except this icing will be made with the Joy of the Lord, and the cake will fill us with peace knowing Jesus is making us well again.

CHAPTER THIRTEEN
Senses

I 'VE NEVER HAD a problem in a failing sort of way, but rather my senses seemed to enhance and be connected to the point of hypersensitivity. Don't ask me to make sense (no pun intended) because like the other body mysteries, I don't know how to solve them.

But I will go through them, one at a time, going over what I live with the best I can.

My hearing seems to be connected to the way my mind works, or in certain sounds, noises, does not work. For example, I can't write, read, or talk in a room with other sounds, TV, someone talking on the phone, phones ringing, or a room that echoes. Certain sounds seem to irritate me more than others, but that could be from weak adrenals not able to tolerate stress. But with a pair of good sound-blocking headphones, and listening to music, I am better able to focus my mind.

My sight is good, except when it comes to bright or flashy lights. Or with TV people wearing the wrong shirts that become flashy lights on camera. Like my hearing, my sight also has a hypersensitivity that connects to my mind and the way I can or cannot focus. Sunglasses help, but I've yet to find a pair that's just right like the headphones. Just doesn't help with my peripheral vision, and in the background vision, even though probably why I'm so observant in being distracted by movement.

My sense of smell has always been sensitive even as a kid. From being able to smell daddy long-leggers, to smelling my Dad's breath (sorry Dad, but back then I had to hold my breath when talking to you face-to-face).

I don't know how Babiesa affected my smell, except I think my nose sensitivity increased. For example, the smell of wet clothes just out of the washing machine gives me a headache the same way a hot wood stove does. I definitely can't handle stinkbugs, have to wash my hands until the smell leaves.

I sometimes was asked to smell stuff because of my strong sense of smell to identify what it was, like if I smelled gas I was asked one time at my Aunt's.

Like my hearing, sight, my sense of smell also connected to my sensitive mind that kept me from concentrating, but there's nothing I can do except leave, move away from the smells that bother me. Because I needed my nose clear for breathing, especially when sleeping.

Getting a stuffy nose was the worst, even when it meant dealing with bad smells. Can't focus, couldn't sleep in a hot room with a stuffy nose. Not to mention getting dry and getting a lot of nose bleeds through the years. But the nose bleeds could have been from deficiencies in Vitamins, specifically vitamin C which I have found is easy to do when not getting the whole complex and taking just synthetics. The good news is my nosebleeds have gotten a lot better since doing intermittent fasting and ketosis.

My sense of taste buds probably gets me more in trouble, because of giving me the love for foods, and the combinations of textures. Once I find a taste that I love I have a hard time stopping until I've had my fill. I have a hard time watching TV shows with food, because it builds up that desire to experiment with my own textures with food.

My weakness was chocolate and peanut butter. Luckily for me, I found them sugar free. But still, I had to remember just because my taste buds liked something didn't mean my digestion did also.

I find it interesting how the senses connect to the mind besides the neurons transmitting back to the brain. Even the sense of taste with smells get back to the mind, either wanting more, or having enough. The danger is, and the habit I've often fallen into, is deciphering between satisfying for pleasure, and satisfying an addiction.

If you can give something up for a few weeks then you're good, but if not, you might have to stop buying it, and use something else to rid of the aftertaste that we don't like.

My sense of touch I've not really thought about much. I guess when using something all the time, it can be taken for granted. Except when it came time for feeling the tightness bringing on the pain even though feeling pain can be a good thing when it's a warning to stop and back off. As far as the sense of touch is related to Babiesa, I've yet to figure that one out. Where do Babiesa symptoms begin first? And then where do they end after going unnoticed for 23 years? Yes, I knew in my sixth or seventh sense which ever the listing to the gut falls into. Unless heightened emotions are part of the sense of touch. The kind of emotions I've tried hiding in the back of my inner thought closet until the doors couldn't be closed anymore until they busted through.

As for my sense of mind, I just can't seem to turn it off, whether it has resulted from Babiesa or too much sugar over the years. It takes a long time, it seems, after hitting the pillow, to sleep. So many conversations within my mind over stuff that never comes to pass. One of the reasons why I stopped watching TV after nine pm: I might start winding down sooner. I'm still experimenting on what relaxes my mind best.

I don't know about anyone else, but I love my sleep except when satan tries sneaking into my dreams. It's why I pray every night before trying to sleep. I ask the Lord to guard my mind and my dreams.

I also need to learn to pray the same during the day when I'm wide awake, because satan will try breaking into our mind every chance given. It's why it's important to get the mind deep into God's Holy Word daily and nightly.

What is amazing is how the mind also affects the other senses. The mind is a power we really shouldn't underestimate. Because the Truth is, everything in our body is connected to our senses and to our mind. I'm not a medical genius, or a rocket scientist. Just from reading God's Word, I get that God didn't miss a single detail in making our host bodies a house for our soul.

Even though it took awhile, I am now grasping how complex God made our bodies to function. The thing is, if we allow our minds to reach ruin, (blaming satan only goes so far; not as far, however, as sticking to our No) our bodies will follow suit. It's why we have to think positively and spiritually.

Negative thinking will start stressing the adrenals and the rest of the body, not to mention getting into bad eating habits. I'm speaking of the body's connection to the mind, but we can lack communication about what we're deficient in.

For example, when lacking potassium, the body will send signals noting a need for something sweet. With our mind in the food gutter, we think it means we need to eat sugar. In fact, it means we need to eat the opposite, more vegetables.

By the way, too much sugar also causes mood swings in the mind. Learning about the senses and how everything in the body works together is something I found out the hard way, and I'm hoping my mistakes will help others to learn from them.

CHAPTER FOURTEEN
Hypersensitivity

BABIESA – OR AGAIN too much sugar – caused my sensitivity to become hyperactive. I can only guess from what I have to go on, and from what I've been learning.

The hypersensitivity has caused me to hit the breaks in other areas of my life. Like, for example, the way I speak in order for my thoughts to form the right words, instead of rushing them before thinking things through. When at a Bible study, or church, I often don't answer the questions. A few days later, once I have processed the words, I do in poem form. I want my words to make sense.

My heightened sensitivity wants to be the hare, when I need to be the tortoise, in order to win over my thoughts before turning them into actions.

More times than not, unfortunately, it is the hare racing in my mind that jumpstarts my sensitivity to certain things around me, like noises, distracting lights. I probably look more serious on the outside when in public because I try extra hard to keep the tortoise pace rather than run like the hare, as I often do when at home.

I hope, pray, if parents are reading my book, that they

take serious notes when I talk about how sugar affected me. Even if Babiesa played a part, so did too much sugar and too few vegetables.

Learn to start reading labels, the ingredients like the Bible, and learn to recognize the hidden words for demons, I mean sugar. Once again, blaming the companies only goes as far as sticking to our No.

The more we stick to our Nos, to what we won't allow to come into our bodies. Hopefully, more companies will start taking notice. The same goes with the drug making companies. We need real food, less frequently.

In other words, stop grazing like cows, and start grazing like human tortoises, slowly until our stomachs catch up to our minds or vice versa. A properly fed, working body will help slow the hypersensitivity down. A poorly-fed, non-working body will give the mind Hyperactive Disorder, as the label for consuming too much sugar goes.

Of course, blaming the sugar companies only goes so far as the No and the greed paid off from the companies. But still, learn to slow down and let the No win. Be more mindful of what goes in, and learn through what comes out of our bodies in order to treat the main issue and not just the symptoms.

CHAPTER FIFTEEN
Symbolism

I'VE ALWAYS HAD trouble explaining things so others could understand what I'm going through, the way that I think and do things, the way I see things in my mind don't always come out in words from mind to mouth.

Whether because of stuttering, or my mouth just not opening wide enough when I talk. When distracted by the sounds around me it's hard for me to focus my thoughts on the right words.

I also have trouble pronouncing certain words, especially big words, and if I can't pronounce I can't always remember. My mind works better when learning visually, through visions in daydreams, but I can't always interpret my visions into words unless I have music to unlock them.

I can't listen to music and talk using my voice at the same time, however, because I need to hear myself. This is why my conversations are short and to the point when in public with other loud sounds, talking.

Unless led to talk about certain topics, I have a hard time completing my thoughts clearly enough to pick one. My thoughts are so random it's like my thoughts have ADHD. This is just the way God made my mind to work, maybe it's my sixth sense, a gift I'm still learning to use.

For the past few of my books, I've been trying to add photos with symbolism to show what my view in visions kind of looks like. For example, in the book *Midnight Ride Of The Son* I used photos that symbolized a rider like the Lone Ranger that was on a mission, except it represented Jesus coming to save us before the second coming.

In the book *Love Intertwined* I used photos that symbolized Love being alive, that Love is an extension of God just like the Holy Spirit.

1 John 4:8 "Anyone who does not love does not know God, because God is love." Through this extension we're connected to how and why God Loves us, to not to understand Love, but to understand more of who we're Created to be, which enables us to figure out who we're to Love, and how we're to love them until death do us part.

In this book I've used photos that symbolize what it's kind of been like in my shoes, that symbolize how I've felt alone in my thoughts until God puts visions in my mind, which parallels the images of contained leaves instead of scattered ones, leading me to answers or, more importantly, reminding me of Who has them and is still in control, reminding me to keep looking up, focusing on Jesus Christ, and trusting Him to lead me, instead of trying to go my own way.

Even though we all may feel alone in the boat in the middle of the biggest ocean, we're not alone, just like the wind can't be felt or be seen until we see leaves being swept up.

CHAPTER SIXTEEN
Outbursts

One symptom I rarely mentioned was my emotional outbursts
Snapped at little things, never in public, but frustrations at home
Would feel so guilty while wondering why I did what I did

Biggest pain from undiagnosed Lyme disease isn't physical
But emotional guilt for lashing out or shaking at those you love
Feeling like a crazy monster was the worst pain of all

Time after time was asked why I acted all angry like at home
Which gave me plenty of time in my closed room to reflect
Couldn't figure out the why, so just talked to God

Year after year, everything got worse, legs quicker to tighten
Forearms tightening kept me from working with my hands
Fingers would go numb from holding the fork too long

Biggest pain from undiagnosed Lyme disease isn't physical
But pain nobody, but God can see behind the lonely eyes
Because of not able to explain what I felt walking in my shoes

Wasn't until I got medical assistance since I lost insurance at 18
That finally could start trying to find answers, to my body not working
But by then my weight gaining was too much to be overlooked

Not one doctor gave me answers, just more questions and medication
That caused me to gain more weight, which led to obesity being
diagnosed
But was told the rest was me being normal, another false label

Thank God for the dogs he sent me, for speaking to me through music
Writing poetry gave me purpose, peace of mind, even through my pain
Thought it be worth it if I could ease someone else's pain

Since nobody understood what my body was going through
I just adapted best I could, learned what slowed contractions
Why I only wear shorts, because of tightening on leg contact

Games, TV became my way of escaping so tired of contracting muscles
Food became my medication for emotional frustration and pain relief
Not being able to exercise, weight became even more of a burden

Stuttering didn't help, just another label, a confidence stealer
Another symptom that gets own referral for speech therapy
Nobody thought to add symptoms up or put them together

Getting diabetes became more of a blessing than a burden
Helped me to read labels in eating better, result of losing weight
But didn't matter what I'd lose, eventually gain all back

Golf was the only thing keeping me from going crazy
Gave me an outlet for frustrations, something I could do
Thank God for golf carts so I didn't walk until feet went numb

Through all the years God has been good to me, providing needs
Helping my Faith get stronger with every broken, pained step taken
Speaking words of poetry for me to write

After all these years of undiagnosed, 1000 prayers said for healing
God provided the way using my Uncle's wedding to see my Great Cousin
Who gave me what no doctor has given me, right diagnosis, answers to pain

Took 24 years to find it's been parasites all these years of Lyme disease
Part of me wants to be angry, but the Faith in me knows it was God's plan
Like He used the Thorn in the side of Apostle Paul
Don't know how long the road to recovery will take me, don't know the stops
But I look forward to what God has to give me along the way to being healed
With one faithful step at a time will get there

Looking back with all the people I've touched, books of poetry written
Don't know if I'd want anything changed not even the pain felt inside

Because it's what God used to help me make a difference

God has been so faithful, watching every step I take, so I don't fall
Providing every dog I've needed to remind me to be calm, be still
God is watching so do not worry He will provide to do His will

Biggest pain from undiagnosed Lyme disease isn't physical
But it doesn't matter anymore because God's grace is enough
Who needs normal, all we need is Humility and His love

CHAPTER SEVENTEEN
Secret Battles

YOU WON'T FIND a lot of pictures of me after age 20. Some will say it's because I hated my picture taken. But the truth is, it wasn't the picture taken itself, but rather my view of the picture that I hated.

I don't know if it was a lack of confidence in myself because of trying to please others especially ones I looked up to like my Dad and always feeling of coming up short of their expectations of me.

The mystery of my body getting worse never helped, coming up short of a task, even simple ones because my legs, arms just wouldn't let me. I've really had no clue of what part of me worked and didn't work after 10 minutes of use. I was lost and confused as to what I could do with my life that my body would let me do. Thankfully God gave me the gift of poetry and sent me online friends to talk to.

Then of course I couldn't stop gaining weight after age 28. I struggled not hating myself every time I looked in the mirror even though I knew God made me like this for a reason. Reading this book, one might think I was depressed, and maybe I was. After age 35, all I focused on was trying to lose weight and to sift through all the advice; trying to figure what would work for me. Feeling pressure from others, let alone myself was stressing me. Lazz and Bosley both became like me as I shared my bad eating habits with them.

I'm just sharing beyond the poetry and when I was playing golf, listening to music and talking with my Grandfather, I struggled finding myself, but as my faith grew more and more, after each published book even though I felt lost in myself, even in my distractions. I started seeing myself in Psalm 139, and how God made me perfect just the way I am. He doesn't make flaws.

I was lost in finding my dream, and somewhere down the line, after age 35, I stopped dreaming of riding on horseback to my favorite places in the Mountains. I stopped dreaming about adventures, in general, and probably because I had stopped reading my favorite books. I didn't feel like reading, and maybe that was depression.

My Babiesa symptoms affected how I felt. For sure, I was frustrated and just plain tired. In my mind, frustration and depression could feel the same way, though, because every time I shared my story with anyone, especially with doctors, I felt like I was going unheard, never understood, that all my symptoms got swept under the rug, treated as one.

As the years passed, and as I learned to adapt to everything, my body continued to go through changes. It's why I stopped wearing pants after 2008, even in the winter.

Besides I had trouble finding ones that fit. The materials got my legs warm too fast, causing the contractions, and I just started doing every little thing that slowed my muscle contractions, plus my legs never really got cold, my feet did, but not my legs. The comments I received back especially in winter got old, and got a few jokes, but if they only walked in my shoes I'd thought but never said anything.

I'd also watch where I walked, more bumpy the ground, more up hill the more, I started sitting in church during prayer and worship, plus for whatever reason I feel I'm losing my balance when my eyes are closed standing up. I was doing everything I could to delay the pain I knew was coming.

How much of what I was going through was simply my head – whether Babiesa, or too much sugar – and how much of it was satan fighting me? Only God knows. Thankfully, God still used me through all of this, like He used Rich Mullins.

We've all got battles we're ashamed to share with people. I don't want to admit satan is in my head. But if satan didn't try getting in, it would have meant we're not doing enough to build the Kingdom of God.

We might not know God's reason for letting us go through these battles, but we should know by now that we're not alone, and I'm not just talking about God. I'm also talking about other brothers and sisters in the Lord that need help getting through these battles.

If they don't see us getting through spiritual, physical, and mental battles, how will they find the hope to keep fighting? This is why I'm sharing my stories in this book now, and, just to be crystal clear, I'm not doing this book to blame anyone.

I'm just sharing what I was going through and what I have overcome. I have found the courage and confidence to share how God used my open wounds to come inside and heal me.

I wasn't healed through more medication, but through faith and trust in Jesus Christ, Who has used other people coming into my life to show me the Answers that reside in Him and through foods He Created naturally, as He designed them to help us grow stronger.

Satan wants us to use God's Creation, by trying to change it or re-create it for a cheaper version, and make money in the process. But unfortunately, like Adam and Eve found out, like all non-repentant sinners will discover, we can't make it without God providing exactly what our bodies need, without spiking a chemical, or hormone imbalances that make the bodies' defenses weaker, which allows viruses to come back alive.

Living by the Truth might be more expensive than the synthetic (interesting how synthetic is so close to sinthetic), but living cheaply is not beneficial, like the real Way of living for Jesus Christ and living off His nature like He intended for us to live. What we get for free in life doesn't mean there won't be a cost paid at some point down the road. It's just a matter of who pays that price. Despite one little bite of forbidden fruit that we tried to hide from God, we're given a gift the eternal life. The gift wasn't free. The blood of the Son of God, Jesus Christ, paid for it.

Thankfully, secret battles can come to the Light and be as

finished as Jesus made our Salvation when the stone was rolled away and Jesus walked out of the tomb on the third day.

I have overcome my battles through the healing of Jesus. I truly believe the plan He laid out for me to follow will be for His Glory just as He designed since my birth.

Working through His details was up to me, in order to shine His Light through the roughness of storms in the dead of night, to see that Jesus is here guiding us.

If only we'd use our faith and trust in Him enough to obey and only eat what He gives us, drink from His well, follow His way to a blessed life.

CHAPTER EIGHTEEN
Mystery Not Solved

I COULDN'T ANSWER many things, even if I wanted to, because it's the mystery of me that I don't know. Maybe my liking to look for details was passed on through my DNA from my Creator, the God of Love, and of details.

I don't know why my nose is so sensitive to certain smells that lead to nauseous pain and eventually headaches. I don't know why my hearing is sensitive to noises. I don't know why little things bother me to the point of becoming a big deal.

But maybe God gave me this attention to detail as part of my gift to write poetry, because it's in the details I find the inspiration to look for the words that match those inside my head, to assemble stanzas until lines of three are written down six to seven times.

Through all of my years, I tried to understand the mystery of me, and why I am made like I am.

The Answer came very clear to me in my present state of mind. I don't need to understand the mystery of me, and who I am. The Answer is to accept who I am, and Whose I am, while being thankful He chose me to be the way that I am.

Yes I may have flaws, weaknesses that satan tries to

exploit everyday, every night. But I have a Savior that I call on daily to rebuke satan, and I feel the peace and stillness of only Jesus can bring, and it is He that only belongs in me.

Like 2 Corinthians 12:10esv says "For the sake of Christ, then, I am content with weaknesses, insults, hardships, persecutions, and calamities. For when I am weak, then I am strong."

2 Corinthians 12:7-10msg says it this way: "Because of the extravagance of those revelations, and so I wouldn't get a big head, I was given the gift of a handicap to keep me in constant touch with my limitations. Satan's angel did his best to get me down; what he in fact did was push me to my knees. No danger then of walking around high and mighty! At first I didn't think of it as a gift, and begged God to remove it. Three times I did that, and then he told me, My grace is enough; it's all you need. My strength comes into its own in your weakness. Once I heard that, I was glad to let it happen. I quit focusing on the handicap and began appreciating the gift. It was a case of Christ's strength moving in on my weakness. Now I take limitations in stride, and with good cheer, these limitations that cut me down to size— abuse, accidents, opposition, bad breaks. I just let Christ take over! And so the weaker I get, the stronger I become."

Some mysteries don't need to be understood, just accepted as part of Whose we are. We don't need to understand the mystery of who we are, just accepting of who God is making us to be. The body that our soul rests in is only part of how God formed us in our Mothers' womb.

Sure, I may have come out with tight joints and ligaments. Sure, I may have grown up the way I did with short, high arched feet that have a hard time finding shoes to fit in. Sure, at some point a tick decided to pick me to be attached to unknown or believed by anyone for the next twenty-four years. Sure, I might have had the flu around that time, the only time, with a host of other symptoms that can't be connected like dots back to the origins, to where and what it all began from. But it was through these circumstances that God chose to continue Creating who I am today.

The birth was only the beginning of forming the host, to house my soul that needed a residence of Jesus to feel at home in a rental. The pain I felt all of those years wasn't from being broken, but from Jesus tweaking me where He needed to help my already broken body mend.

Don't you know most pain isn't from the breaking itself, but from the repairing, putting our brokenness back in place.

Some of our brokenness needed screws to hold the most messed up parts in place, like a doctor uses a screw to hold the broken bones in place. What gets done to us, by who or whatever, is unfortunate, but doesn't keep us broken. No, we ourselves keep us from being healed by not forgiving what was already done. Holding back bitterness is the infection that produces fever like in the body, except it produces hate in the soul and heart.

We need to accept the forgiveness that comes from Jesus and extend the forgiveness towards those we think hurt us to let the healing of our brokenness continue.   The character building God is doing, comes from His healing, from putting us back together until our Healing is complete, and we're free to leave our rental home, and free to go back to Eden, our Home in Heaven where we belong beside our Father and Jesus.

We're all different with different likes. Sometimes we have similarities to offset our differences. But God needs us different for reasons He only knows, and we don't need to understand, just accept that we're His and He loves us exactly the way we are, and obey, just like He designed every detail that came to be us.

I wish I could remember more in detail of my stories, but I spent so long trying to forget the pain, to hide from the pain, that I lost sight of God using those times to heal me, work through me.

So now that I have found the healing that I sought for and have realized the revelation about the journey of self-discovery that I've been on, so that I can have the courage to go back through the painful memories and share my stories, even though some are lacking details. I hope the fog has cleared enough to show that God wasn't just talking to the Apostle Paul in 2 Corinthians, but talking to us as well. That the Grace of Christ Jesus is enough, we don't need anything else to thrive in this world.

There are no limitations to what the Grace of Christ can do, and will do, so that His Glory can be seen overcoming anything that the world has to offer good or bad. I could have played the blame card, might sound like I'm blaming

Doctors to some, but I am just telling my story as I learned to deal with everything. I know we're all human, and we can only go by what we know. Sure could be better prepared as life changes that make the circumstances.

In the end, the choice how to proceed with what we've been told is up to us. Either accept the advice and treatment suggestions, or have the courage to say no, I'm going to try it a different way. Again, though, in the end, live with the consequences, with the choices made. Better yet, learn to trust in Jesus more, and leave the consequences up to Him.

Trusting Jesus more and more each day, pain or no pain, I chose to give thanks instead of getting mad at God for allowing me to go through hard times.

I rebuke satan when thoughts of doubt and blame try sneaking in my mind and heart. Learn to pray through these times while trusting on the Lord's timing to answer, and, in the meantime, clean out anything in the heart that keeps us from praising, worshipping the Lord with a pure and thankful heart.

CHAPTER NINETEEN
What Ifs

WHAT IFS GO through my mind a lot, especially the fear of missing opportunities because of my physical problems. Hearing I was still young when searching for an in-person girlfriend never really made me feel better. Hearing if only you could drive despite my leg issues, despite my forearm issues, made me think inside, 'if you walked in my shoes, used my body'. Maybe those that said that knew what I was going through.

Yet at the same time voices in my head said, What if they're right? Was it doubt, fear keeping me from being able to do better? Even though I told myself it's not fear for me, but fear for them when I lose control. I just didn't understand what was going on with my body before I knew it was Babiesa Lyme, though I'm sure my eating habits had something to do with my physical problems.

Through the years, in searching for answers, doctors asked me if I was feeling depressed. I honestly didn't know how to answer. Although I was afraid of more prescribed medication if I said yes. Was I, am I having trouble deciding if I was happy or sad? Yes I was, but I didn't know how to tell which was frustration from lack of real answers from anyone.

Or was I so lost, I literally didn't know what happiness felt like, because, to be honest, I didn't know if I was feeling anything at times. I was even getting to the point of not knowing what my dreams were anymore.

Because I was so tired of the physical limitations, so tired of taking one step forward, three steps back in weight loss. The only thing I know was giving me true joy, was writing poetry for Jesus Christ and the occasional trip to the golf course, where I could get lost anywhere but my pain. When I could think of playing golf, I could let my head take a break from getting lost in my what if thoughts.

Thankfully, God knows what we're going through. God knows about our limitations, and knows He can do more with them than what we think. After all, God allows us to go through these circumstances to work on our trust, to trust Him enough with our obedience to work through those circumstances anyway.

While I was trying to figure out how to get through with my physical problems He was using them to build my character. Even though I doubted at times, faith wasn't as strong, I did use those circumstances to humble myself.

Every time someone drives me anywhere it's humbling, even though I have to remind myself I am worth helping. Even though it can be frustrating for them at the same time. But I think it's also God's way of having us humble each other.

We get so busy, with work distractions, we need to remind each other to slow down, remember what we're really doing here, which is helping to build the Kingdom of God through the building up of each other.

Thrive Without Hurt

Everyone wants to thrive, just not going through circumstances
That lead to finding what it takes for us to thrive in this world
Just as long as we don't have to go through the pain to thrive

But we really have to go through the pain in order to find what it takes
What it really means, to what it looks like to thrive instead of struggle
Without the pain we can't build the character to thrive

If only we lived in a world where we didn't have to find answers
Connected to questions we don't understand, and can't move
Until we have the logic to those answers we seek to thrive

But we really have to go through trusting the Answer without logic
That gives us the understanding to why we're going through hell
When we just want to be left alone living our on life for me

Everyone wants to thrive without the benefit of the doubt from you
About the Truth of needing to love each other, with Love from God
We don't want to hear, in order to thrive we need the heart break

But we really have to go through betrayal, the stabbing in the back
So we can truly learn how to forgive, even though it hurts like hell
Because Jesus went through hell to forgive, to save us of our sins

Learning to Love, to forgive no matter the hurt we go through in life
Because face it, falling off the world's pedestal without Jesus hurts
But knowing we got forever living with Jesus will have us thriving
together

Family and I at Golf Tournament

CHAPTER TWENTY
Wonder

SOMETIMES I WONDER if I have additional symptoms because of the Babiesa or poor eating habits. When writing poetry I always have lines of three in each verse. And I have trouble focusing if they go too long, causing a fourth line.

Same can be said about the way I unload the dishwasher in certain order, and, if out of order, I get irritated. I lose focus with too much noise, phone ringing, evening coffee sipping, eating crunchy foods, and certain light colors like on DVRs, blinking red light shoes.

I don't really know why or how to explain when it started. I'm guessing towards my first book with the poetry and everything else. It gradually happened over the last five years. Don't know if it's related to the brain fog that was getting worse past three years.

Thankfully, though, it means I've not lost much hearing from playing loud music through headphones that block out the noise around me, which has helped me think over the years. I believe God's been watching over me, using whatever's going around in my head. Through the music in the headphones, I hear Him – God, the Holy Spirit – it's the only way I can explain how I've written all of these poems over the years. Don't know how else my thoughts clear enough to start picking out words that go with the vision and what's being spoken in my inner ear.

My one friend, Dwayne, after my Grandfather Walker's memorial service, said my poetry reminded him of King David and the way he wrote. So, in a way, after Dwayne told me, I could see the connection. Not that I was running, hiding from a former king trying to kill me. Yet I too was hiding from the pain caused by enemies I couldn't see when writing.

Songs Of Poetry

Songs of poetry music to the ears words spoken to the heart
That's the way I hear it when listening then I the words forming
This is when it's clear to write it down and the spirit has spoken

Gift it is from the Lord to remind us all that He still speaks
If we'll only take the time to listen and pass along His message
Never know when someone needs to hear it that day

Words I hear in the song I am listening to don't always match
This is when I know it is the Lord singing for my heart to hear
He is whispering the message someone needs to hear right now

Somewhere someone needs uplifting, a new message of hope
Some way, some how the words spoken to my heart is related
Never know when someone needs to hear it that day

Songs of poetry music to the ears words spoken to the heart
This is the way the Lord speaks to me through His spirit of song
Just like the way He talked to David a man after His own Heart

5/19/2012
Poem In The Song

Everyone's trying to find the poem in the song
And when they don't find it frustration sets like
The cement covering our hearts giving up hope

Sometimes we write the poem in the song
Other times we become the poem in the song
That sings of His glory, bringing the sun up to rise

We're trying so hard in the dead of night to write words
That will impact the world, win the Pulitzer prize to show
We worked enough to get the salvation Heaven gives

The Song has already written the poem made from His blood
There's nothing left to write that will earn what's already free
The impact will break away the cement covering our hearts

Sometimes we write the poem in the Song
Other times we become the poem in the Song
That sing's of His love that brings out the promise

Everyone's trying to find the poem in the Song
And when they look into the mirror of truth to find
They've been the poem this whole time.

CHAPTER TWENTY ONE
Help

ASKING FOR HELP and accepting help is humbling in different ways.

We first have to swallow pride to admit we don't have the strength, or means, to accomplish the task at hand. And then, secondly, we have to learn to accept the help without the doubt of self worth coming in. Truthfully, accepting help takes humble courage.

Think about Jesus, who could have done the works all by Himself. But Jesus asked 12 disciples to help Him on His journey to the cross. Sure it was probably also so we could know Him. After all, He already knew us. Jesus was teaching us, not only about faith, grace, love and mercy, but also about how to walk with humility.

Thanks to my body being weak, I don't know for sure why. Could've been Babiesa most of my years, or my bad diet creating lack of nutrients. But still God used it to teach me how to be humble. So many times I had to swallow my pride, asking for help in my own way. Fighting off the doubts about self worth was a daily battle. Never able to leave home because I wasn't able to take care of myself enough. Plus not knowing if anyone truly understood what I was going through, let alone what I was feeling.

I just didn't trust, understand my own body enough to be able to drive long enough, safe enough to get anywhere. The fear isn't for my safety, but for others on the road. Yes, I could drive the lawn tractor fine enough, except for the pain, then numbness in my hands. Yes I could drive a golf cart for a time until pain got in my legs, but both times had no traffic. Just had to worry about not tipping over on hills.

But still I get that if I drove life would be easier on everyone, and I hope one day my body will work to the point of not wondering when the pain will come, so I can live normally.

Life really changes when friends get married and move away. Then again, when family starts moving away. Becomes harder to get out of the house because it means swallowing pride a lot and asking for help just for a change from feeling alone with all the thoughts going in and out of my head.

While I was fighting thoughts, feelings satan was feeding about my self worth, God was teaching me, building my character to keep me humble, which I've asked for, because I didn't want to lose the connection to God, the Holy Spirit with my poetry.

I know I am worth it, I know I am Loved. God proved it to me when He sent His Son Jesus to die on the cross for me, and you.

Charlie's Tree

How many of us have walked past the weak looking
Going right for the strongest, the tallest of them all
Never giving the small let alone the average a thought?

Going against the world's choice can be hard, but so can falling
The sudden thud should be a wake up call if it wasn't too far a drop
This is what happens when we climb on shoulders unstable

How many of us have walked passed the weak minded
Going right for the highest IQ the brightest of them all
Never giving the small, let alone the average a thought

Going against the world's logic can be hard, but so is a wall
The sudden thud of running into a dead end should be a clue
This is what happens when we're closed mined and lost

If the world had it's choice David would never have been King
Who was this teen facing a giant, they said, never giving him a chance
But a stone throw later David stood standing over a headless giant

All the Lucys in the world would have wanted us to get a perfect tree
But instead there was One who would get the smallest tree of them all
Yes the world would make fun, but He would remain standing above
them

How many of us will be Charlie Brown and not be chosen by
appearance
But by character, the attributes worthy of Christ, who 2000 years ago
Jesus climbed on a Charlie tree for you and me, we the chosen of God

CHAPTER TWENTY TWO
God-Sent People

OVER THE YEARS I've been learning God sends people into your life at the right time to help your character grow. Sometimes the people come for a time in your life, then when God's purpose for connection with us is complete, they move on.

My first realization that my poetry was a gift came from a friend I met on a Christian forum where I first started sharing poetry. Everhope was her username and she was the first that told me I had the gift and gave me the inspiration to keep writing. Another friend that I met playing online poker was Gigi among a table full of friends. No, it wasn't for the poker I kept coming back to the same online site, but the fellowship of friends.

They're all important to me, but Gigi was like the online Mother full of wisdom, a voice used by the Lord strong in faith. I talked to Gigi as often as I could and she helped me more than she knows. Like the video games, I needed an outlet to distract me from the pain and confusion of the real world. Gigi also helped me to be a better witness, as I initially was strong in the defense of truth, and mistakenly took out my frustration.

Defending

What happens when we as Christians get called something else?
How easy it is to start defending one's reputation than to remember
Who really is trying to get under our skin?

Oh Lord, how I know should have handled the disagreement better
Please teach me how to use these situations for your glory
Even when my honor in their eyes is questioned

Modern day eyes see everything by internet or face to face
How easy it is to be blinded by what we think we see and reality?
Just because of the trespassers that came before, we didn't forgive

Oh Lord, how many times have I read your prayer but forget to use it
Please teach me how to use these situations for your glory not my gain
Even when my honor in their eyes is questioned

Defending the truth of who we are doesn't matter without Love
The importance is knowing God knows we're His and who we are
The truth will be revealed and the attacker will know

If Jesus is for us, who can be against us? Jesus is our defender
With the Lord being our refuge, our strength, our shield, our redeemer
There is no need to defend the names of lies, when Truth stands in
victory

CHAPTER TWENTY THREE
Online Sensitivity

U NFORTUNATELY ONLINE I sometimes came across sensitive, taking things too seriously. Unintentionally, I ended up hurting some of my friends and Gigi helped me learn from those mistakes.

I learned pain could still be felt online not just feeling my pain, but pain I felt when I was causing others to hurt also. The pain was from guilt and I've always had a hard time shaking that kind of pain starting with the letting out of my first dog Zack.

I've blamed myself for a good 20 years. This was why I thought I lost it out of nowhere at home, and was afraid of myself to lose it in public. I did learn short tempers were a symptom of Babiesa Lyme disease, that it wasn't totally me. But the guilt just wouldn't let go of me whenever I lost it, in real life or online.

It was it in this period when I wrote this poem. Even in the darkest moments, the Lord's Light of Truth can be seen.

Should Have Been Mine

Feels like there's a sink hole inside my heart
But the suffering is by my own anguished hands
I deserve nothing more than an eye for an eye

My heart's inside a whirlpool going round and round
Part of me just wants to give up, get quickly sucked in
I deserve nothing more than to suffer tooth for a tooth

I deserve to be buried alive in an avalanche for the suffering I caused
I'd expect nothing less than to be stuck waist deep in my own trap
Just waiting for the snowballs to be thrown wishing they are stones

I deserve nothing more than to burn alive in my own wildfire
Started by my own spark now surrounded by a wall of fire
Just wish the smoke wouldn't knock me out, I deserve to suffer

Why Lord did you take the suffering that I deserve? You didn't do it
I am the one to blame, I deserve to be strung up to die on a tree
But instead it was you on the tree and me holding the hammer

The suffering, the death should have been mine, but you said enough
Through love, mercy and grace the price has been paid with my blood
Together we'll walk out of the depths of the earth

Black And Blue Toes

We're born into this world with narrow vision to the truth
Because of this lack of understanding for a time we're immune
For Jesus loves the little children, but we take this for granted

Before too long we're left stumbling in the dark feeling our way
Only when we stub our toes will we realize this is the wrong way
But some of us refuse to let go of pride and keep trying

We're now lost and wondering why we feel numbness in our walk
Because of this we're on our hands and knees more often than not
Those that have taken advantage will have found the hands to lift them

Before too long we're looking into the eyes of the healer, forgiver of sin

Those that take the hands will be saved and eyes will be open to the light
But some of us will lose zeal and wander back into the dark

We've forgotten though saved by Jesus we're far from perfect till we stumble
Then we cry in anger to God, why the pain, when it's our own toes we stub?
The price we pay is black and blue when getting lost without directions

Jesus is the light and He knows where satan put the traps in the dark
This is why we should follow Him, and not make our own way blindfolded
We're always one step from falling head over heels in a place hard to get up

Thank the Lord for giving toes to stub it's better to get black and blue
Then lose our heads, which we can't get back, only get one in this life
Stop the cursing and praise the Lord for the hand that lifts us up again

Our toes will get black and blue, but the Lord will always be there
Will be lifted up when we stumble, His forgiveness brushes off sin
Just the way it will be until the last sin is covered by His blood

CHAPTER TWENTY FOUR
Online Touch

S OME OF THE poems I have written are about those who I met online, and who have touched me enough to include them in a poem vision.

Sometimes we're the ministers to those we meet online or offline, the people who still have need of hope. If we don't find any to minister to, then maybe we need to be ministered to. The following poems were inspired from those encounters.

11/26/2007
Two Ladies

There were two ladies, one wore yellow, one wore red at a table
Not at just any table, this table you put it all in with no limit
Unknown to them in the stare down over who had best hand

The two ladies from two separate northwest states had more
Than just poker chips on the line, but a friendship to begin
Only God knew how long before they too had realized the beginning

Friends come and go, playing this game called Texas Hold'em
Friendships get tested but the ladies in yellow and red withstood
On the outside may look different, but on the inside much is the same

Both have that knocking on the door of their hearts someone wants in
Who just wants to tell them how much they're loved and how they're worthy

That their value is beyond riches and goes beyond the poker tables

Together walking the path that was created just for them
They both will see the light and shine a path for others
Maybe it'll be now, maybe it'll be later in their lives

When they do will feel like just went all in with everything on the line
With the flop looking good, 10, jack, queen of hearts, with the ace
On the turn, withholding their breath on the river comes the King

3/20/2007
More Than Poker

There's a WildKat playing with a black and blue bird
Although the meow sounds like a roar but cornered
The roar becomes a meow, the eyes start to glow

Gigi is a sweet, sweet lady who cries tears to love songs
Somehow Gigi has tamed the wildkat but still has tender heart
If you listen closely can hear her whisper sweet aww and aww

Then there's Sent out doing his part in keeping America free
While Gigi's be safe or I'll hurt you echoes in his ears, the Navy seal
Dreams of coming home to the girl he loves

Then there's nurse Meg who's a Cajun on the outside an angel on the inside
The third member of the three amigos, one for all and all for one can be heard
When she talks about her daughter May you can see the Love from Heaven

Then there's Dac who's just being Dac and is just so-so on life
On the outside is full of humor and laughter on the inside it's different
That is seen with a brush and a canvas that brings out the candlelight
Then there's me, just trying to find my way trying to make sense
Trying to find a place to fit in among strangers that are no more
One year later I find I couldn't have asked for a better extended family

I just thank the Lord for having Gigi and Kat making me feel at home
For letting the true me come out from hiding which led to more friends
Which led me the way to meet my bride to be

There's more than poker than what the eyes can see with the winning or losing
But by listening to those that are hurting and reaching out a hand of friendship
Showing a heart of love can be all the difference they need to see God's love

Het Lad

Sitting across the table in the party poker room was a wild bunch
But what a time between the pairs, three of a kinds, and flushes
So much more came with the exchanges of poker chips

The avatars were fake, but the people were real
The conversations wasn't just to pass the time
But there was care in every word said

This was how I got to know Dac when we first said het
A mistyped letter became more than just a greeting
But a connection between friends

The people we meet on party poker is like playing with chocolates
Never know what's in them until they show their true inside character
But without having to bite inside I knew Dac was the real deal

Both being artists, me of words, him of canvas and brushes
We had more in common than just humor and quietness
But spoke with conviction like all good men do

This Lady I Call Betty

There was a lady that looked tough as nails
Dressed in a leather jacket and dark sunglasses
But can't always judge a book by the cover

Look inside this lady will find she's more like Betty Boo
Sweet and lovely as can be and most caring like her Mom
Not even her dark shades can hide this from those that look

Those who are fortunate enough to know her as a friend

See more inside this lady I call Betty than in themselves
And if lady only knew herself she would feel Heaven on earth

This what I want you to know lady when you read this poem
Your Mom finding you that day was no accident but was a purpose
There's someone watching you that loves you more than His Angels

The Lord has released heaven's rains on you to wash the hurt away
The time has come to rejoice and live for Him and be glad in the life
The One who came down and died for you has given you to live free

Those who are fortunate enough to know her as a friend
See more inside this lady I call Betty than in themselves
Now she's all lady and not just Betty and her smile shows

High Stakes

Here I am sitting at a table playing for high stakes
Across from me is the Lord of hosts also at the table
The lord of darkness with his dominion left and right

The blinds are set the cards are cut the dealer deals
I am given a pair of deuces the betting now begins
But instead of betting chips was something more
With his snake-like eyes lucifer bets fame and fortune
The King of kings with His piercing eyes staring back
Says I call you got nothing devil

Greed in my eyes I quickly call with sweat running down my face
Dealer lays the flop down Ace, Ace, eight bringing a grin to satan
The face of Christ never flinches, just looks as if into my soul

With the evil grin still on his face father of lies bets with flesh
The Son of God says cant fool me you serpent I'm calling you
Really sweating now with hands shaking I call

The turn comes with another eight and the devil's eye twitches
He says I'm all in I'm betting your soul to be damned forever in hell
The eyes of the perfect Lamb looks at me again calls with sad eyes

My pair of deuces no longer any good staring at the dead mans hand

Shirt now soaked with sweat palms sweaty I now know this is for keeps
All of a sudden I feel a new breath inside and a sense of calm I fold

My fate floating on the river and now in the hands of the Messiah
The dealer lays down another eight and the devil smirks with glee
With beads of sweat on His forehead goes all in life for death

Blood can now be seen on the head of the Holy One and in His eyes
Blood and water also flows at His side holes in His hands and feet
With one last breath says I call

Triumph in the eyes of satan lays down a full house with excitement
Just when the devil thought he won it all the hand of Christ fell down
With new life two Aces were revealed with four of a kind Christ won

Now what if I was you and you were playing against the King of Kings
And the Father of lies would put your hand in that of Christ to be Lord
Or will you be bluffing with your pair of deuces against four Aces

CHAPTER TWENTY FIVE
Friends and Mentors

HANGING AROUND THE right friends growing up was a big help in my upbringing. Everyone needs a Paul to mentor a Silas, who then can mentor a James. I had that starting with going to church, having a pastor's son as a best friend, and other friends with good characters who have grown up into men of God.

Though I must admit some of my challenges began with seeing them grow, drift out of touch, seeing them marry, and me being single, unable to drive.

The time comes, though, when Silas becomes Paul and looks for someone to mentor while finding a new mentor ourselves. We're not meant to carry our burdens alone.

This day in age we need good men of God and mentors. Life's never easy even with technological distractions. But we need to learn that getting to know one another is a journey like the 40 days in the wilderness. Some of us, like me, need to go multiple times in search of where God wants to take us next in building our character into Godly manhood.

Satan knows we need mentors, also knows when to tempt us in our 40 day journey. This is where good upbringing by a Father comes in and good Sunday school teachers that feed us the Love of Jesus, to know the response of Jesus to the devil's temptations is our response too.

We can either come out of the 40 days prepared and closer to God's callings, or we can circle back again till we figure Jesus is the Only Way and will find Him in our mentor.

Raised

A mother ostrich came across an egg, looked abandoned so adopted
She sat on the egg, though not her own, but raised it when it hatched
Even though the baby bird named Spirit looked nothing like her own

How are we to grow when not even knowing who we're to become?
Not that we care when lived as children until the teen years passed
Then every friend has found his or her purpose except us

Being raised a bird of a different feather, yet awkward in its walk
With legs being shorter than the rest of the family that took him in
But everyone was jealous of Spirit's growing wingspan

What are we to do when we don't even know whose we are, let alone
Know how to make something so we're looked up to,
Not down upon as if
Success is earned how others judge us on accomplishments in riches

The Spirit was looking down at its own reflection in a puddle of water
Was startled when a flying bird came down and asked, "Why it was walking
When should be soaring high" Spirit was in awe as this bird looked like Him

The help we need from mentors matters in how we're raised so we grow
Whether from our Fathers or best friends, but someone wiser than us
This is how we keep from wandering away from who we're made to be

Spirit was no ostrich, had no one to tell Him who He really was, an eagle

Instead of running along the ground, should have been flying high
above
But no one taught Spirit how to fly until His mentor came along

Why are we running instead of flying on eagle wings like we're born to
fly?
We're created in God's own image made to soar above the darkest
storms
We need to be reminded every day that Jesus raised us up on His
Spirit wings

40 Days

Know where I was, just don't know where I am going
Sometimes I get so lost in my wilderness that I wander
As if I am doing my own 40 days of finding myself

We all have our own wilderness called life to wonder
Some of us find a way out sooner, others take longer
Either way will come out changed better or for worse

Life circumstances tend to dictate where we want to go
Bad days we want to quickly end, good days to go on forever
Things happen out of our control and we don't like losing control

Even Jesus wandered in the wilderness not to find himself
But to prepare Himself for what was to come, to endure sacrifice
Though tempted He stayed on the direction He was meant to take

God allows circumstances in our lives to mold us, mend us
We're not wandering lost as we might think in the wilderness
But following the path He wants us to take in making us who we are

CHAPTER TWENTY SIX
Work

I F I COULD work it would either be on the golf course or if I had the money I'd open up my own little restaurant that would help educate people on what they eat and why. While at the same time showing the pleasures in real food. Golfing, cooking, and writing poetry while spending time with Bosley have been my happy places, things I love doing, but not quite ready to be able to do them all the time when I want to.

I still can only stir something for five minutes at a time, or pet Bosley (not at the same time, don't be silly that's Bosley's job) without my forearm getting tight until they hurt. Would be hard for me to write my own cookbook, because with the creative mind God has given me, I've used it to make up my own dishes. I don't measure anything, just add spices, herbs, seasoning here and there, feeling my way around the dish I'm preparing, just like the way a poem comes to mind.

The Structure is preset with instructions, but the inner design becomes my own. At the end of my book I have added some recipes with the structure laid out, but leaves the design up to you in how you rearrange the seasonings you like. I started cooking my dishes using every vegetable even starchy ones, like corn and potatoes, but all that changed once I learned about insulin resistance and what food combinations spike insulin the most, what's high on the glycemic index.

I started adapting my kale stew from adding normal, to being selective towards the Ketogenic lifestyle Dr. Berg's way with lots of green vegetables, only started adding green peas (high vegetable in sugar but good fiber, but still too much sugar for a diabetic) when I got closer to one meal a day.

Learning about the food that I eat has made a big difference in my journey to healing, and as I get closer to my big goal I hope to be taken more seriously. Not taking health class serious enough and not learning how my body works has been one of my regrets.

I try not doing the ifs in life, but when I do I think what would have changed if only I knew back then what I know now. Watching people eat used to fascinate me, the way God made everyone different, the way they worked their bone structure.

But lately, after learning how to spot how to tell if someone has insulin resistance, which means diabetes, watching what people do (no offense) makes me wonder how aware they are of what's going on inside of them.

I don't mean to go on a rant again, but I'm sorry our health care system is such a bad joke that's not funny, but sad at how greed has taken priority over making people well. Sure companies may say it's about saving the consumer money by using synthetics instead of nutrients from real food, but in the end they save money on material resources to make more products that get us hooked, that don't really make us well, just addicted while our bodies suffer and stop making its needed production of the real thing. I'm just sharing my opinion of what I see and read.

I encourage you to take your own journey of discovering truth about what drugs you really need to be taking and if it's for health or for profit? And if you can get the same results of a pill with real food, from vegetables, fats, cholesterol the stuff our bodies are made out of, and need to make more, and repair what was damaged by too much sugar. Learn about the foods you should be eating. Learn to ask the paid by the drug companies experts why they give such recommendations and what real studies did they do? Ask where they learned what?

Obesity is a symptom of ignorance and a sin of gluttony from ignoring the Truth of the real problems for far too long, same with type 2 diabetes. Our digestion plays a big role in our health and healing. If not corrected properly, it will break down, and, when broken, systems start failing, starting with broken defenses.

I believe if everyone would do intermittent fasting and ketosis, two or three months, maybe four, a year, depending on how bad the eating habits are, they would give their bodies a chance to reset and heal.

But breaking the food addictions, drink addictions (yes, I'm talking about alcohol consumption) will be a big step for a journey of better health. Want to solve disease, Cancer, all sickness mysteries, ALS, Dementia, Alzheimer's? Then start with the research of the truth about the consumption of sugar and how everything we ingest is 10 times more than what our bodies can handle let alone take what the body calls toxic.

Start supporting those that raise, grow, handle food the right way, the way God intended us to, maturely and responsibly. Nutrients start from the ground up in the circle of life, the way God intended through the soils of His Creation to benefit His most Loved, you and me.

CHAPTER TWENTY SEVEN
Church

I USED TO love going to church at Grace Fellowship York, though started going when I was in an old Red Lion school hanging out with friends through the youth years listening to music and especially listening to the Pastor's sermons, and Sunday school teachings.

I also loved watching my friend Josh (partner in book making) draw. He's the best I ever saw, and I love the way he brought the art to life. But after I graduated, I did kind of feel a bit lost in a big church, not because of the church itself, but because of what I now know was Babiesa symptoms, especially my leg contractions, which made it hard getting around.

I tried joining the sound crew and would record the sermons once a month and help clean up until legs hurt too much. A few times I did sound for the ladies group on Tuesdays.

Unfortunately, it got to be too much dealing with my body issues and so I stopped doing sound. I tried going to adult after graduation classes, but the walk got tiring for my legs, plus never really made any new friends and my old friends stopped going to Grace. I still loved hearing the music and the sermons, hearing Pastor Larry who I had gotten to know going to a few Baltimore Orioles games and considered Him a friend and Mentor.

After Pastor Larry retired, I struggled going to church for physical and personal reasons with both of us going through transitions, but mostly physical for a few years.

I started having church at home Sunday mornings. Number one, it was easier on my legs plus for whatever reason I was getting back pain in the mornings too painful for church, but it would go away by the afternoon.

I just wanted to be at church when I can focus on the sermon and I love hearing from Pastor Mike. There were just some mornings when I'd try going to church, but only able to stand up for at most one song and have to listen during the praise and worship. Then I'd stand one last time during the meet and greet, then sat during the rest of the service, by the halfway point in the sermon my back would start hurting and I would be praying my back pain to go away instead of hearing the sermon.

So if you saw me one Sunday and not the next for a few weeks, sometimes months, it was never personal, just my physical problems acting up, too much pain.

It was also the reason you saw me dressed in shorts even during the dead of winter, because I preferred being comfortable plus I tried delaying the coming pain long as possible, and it was the cold that kept the pain away, plus with Babiesa my lower legs didn't feel cold until 15 minutes of being outside below 40 degrees.

I would go to Grace every Sunday if I physically could and I pray one day I have no physical issues keeping me away. I love the worship music, even if I don't sing, I just prefer worshiping Jesus in my own way, plus again same problem in my legs is in my arms, just keep my arms raised for long, but praise God He sees our hands raised on high from our rested raised up hands on our knees. I hear God speak to me during every sermon from Pastor Mike, and I've used these teachings as inspiration for my poems.

I know and can feel the Holy Spirit lock these Truths in the back of my mind vault to be used when the time called for those Truths to be used. Just like I believe it's been for every teaching I've heard, I could feel the Holy Spirit at work, even during the times I was in pain.

Maybe I could call it my Grandfather gene passing along the love of healing, the words of God being preached. I truly do thank all the Pastors that were used in passing along God's message. I also thank all the worship leaders at Grace, your voices are truly God's medicine.

CHAPTER TWENTY EIGHT
Relationship with Jesus Christ

MY RELATIONSHIP WITH Jesus Christ means everything to me. Without Him, I'd have no visions for poetry, which I truly believe come from His Holy Spirit.

I'd be so focused on the music I was listening to, deep in my dream Adventures even though always had a different face don't know why, maybe even the face of Christ because in all honesty and speculation I've not seen this face anywhere else except in visions in my dreams. But I'd be in the middle of the latest rescue of a damsel in distress when the words to the song I'd be listening to changed out of the blue.

Then all these words started pumping in my mind and I'd have to run, literally run, to the computer and put on headphones to tune out all outside noise, distractions from hearing the message I was to write out, what I know today as Sonnet Poetry.

I would be so transfixed with words I never even thought of using. Grammar and spelling were the worst subjects I had in homeschooling. Yet here I'd be typing these words until I had 7 to 10 verses depending on how much God wanted me to say, and, yes, I know it was God because of the matching message in His Holy Word even though I can't remember specific numbers and chapters.

The peace of the Lord was with me, and when I'd finish a poem I'd be so drained, I felt like taking a nap. Then I'd share the poem as is, never changing when I felt the Holy Spirit say it was finished. And BTW I'd also had no clue why I was writing what, until someone replied this poem was talking about me today. Or I needed to hear this exact message to lift me up.

Now that I've written so many poems and looked back on them, they could have been for me too, lifting me up, as if saying with Jesus there is more to my life than meets anyone's eye.

Ever since I started believing my gift came from God my Father, Jesus Christ, the Son of God, the Holy Spirit, whichever name you prefer to use, but I use them all because He comes in my storms that could have drowned me, kept me from getting out of the boat, even though fear is in me. My faith in Jesus was always there to calm the storm, or strengthen my faith enough to walk on troubled waters.

Jesus did so through the music coming out of my headphones, or music coming out of the stereo at home or in the car. I'd be listening while praying for the wisdom to hear the next message poem He wanted me to write. Whatever was happening inside my body, whether from Babiesa or from consuming too many carbs on a regular basis, I now know God was not only using my body weakness to defeat distraction and strengthen our relationship, but God was also using me to help others.

If I wasn't home, I don't know if anyone else would listen to other's issues they were dealing with that day. I just happened to be channeling the frequency of God and helping them to hear Him.

Without music in my ear to help me focus to block out noises that distract me, I'd be lost for words and lost for confidence, lost for simple Answers. But with a keyboard at my fingertips, I could use my faith and my newfound confidence. With my newfound confidence, I had to be careful not to collide with my daily frustrations and mood swings that I would take out on others online.

Thankfully, I've been forgiven, 1 John 1:9. The hats you will see me wear are more than fashion, and, to be honest, I used to just wear them for comfort. They made me feel less nervous around people, and I could think a little clearer.

God uses the messages on the hats I wear to remind me of who I am and what He's done. I pray that I apply those Scriptures in my daily walk with Jesus Christ. I'm not just trying to wear Christianity on my sleeve. I'm trying to show it's coming out of my heart, and what's seen on my sleeve is from the overflow coming out. The poetry I've always written has always come from the message received inside my heart, which I've always truly believed, because my life's meaningless without the life of Jesus Christ inside. I would have crumbled, given up long ago, but because of Jesus working through my daily struggles, with my struggles, my daily breakdowns in anger, you name it, that has to do with anything to block pain, that wasn't sin.

Even though I did slip into sin, Jesus was using me, living through me enough for me to refuse to quit. Sure I might retreat, keep trying something until I found something that worked. But I've been knocked down, and gotten up time after time. Lost battle after battle, but I've kept going, because I knew with Jesus my Savior we'd win the war. I knew one day, someday the million prayers I said to be healed, to be normal, healthy would come to pass just like He Promises (Isaiah 53:5), but I was trusting in God's timing.

There were days I doubted, but James 1 would remind me once again to trust Him, to be faithful, and faithful He is. I knew when God was done using me through body pain, to help others I'd be healed only to help others through my inspiration to keep helping others through my ministry of the heart.

My reward has never been about money, even though I wished I'd eventually have made enough just to get by. I just wanted people to read my books anyway God chose to reach out to them.

I don't like charging people to buy my books because of not wanting cost to be a factor in reaching broken hearts. But being on disability income makes giving away books hard to do. Marketing and promoting my books is the hardest part about making my books. I never know what to say in order to sound like I really want to sell my books, and of course my legs keep me from walking up to people and talking to them with confidence that I wouldn't stutter.

So sometimes I ask God who to give them to and just place a book in front of them and walk away letting God do the rest. Pastors, teachers, other believers need to hear encouragement, reminders of why Jesus is working through them.

The relationship I have grown with Jesus over the years from everything I've dealt with is what I've treasured the most, whether it's from listening to music or through my fury friends that has kept me going along with friends I've met over the years online. God is good all the time. I just have to keep looking up, KLU.

Where I Pray

CHAPTER TWENTY NINE
Summarized Journey

If I could summarize this book into one poem
It would start with getting on my knees for help
Every time I went into my prayer closet

There's no doubt about it we need help to discover
That if we don't accept all the help God gives us
Then will be lost wondering in the wilderness

Even though I was walking in pain, I wasn't walking alone
Jesus was right there to lean on, or to even be carried on
Doesn't matter how we get there, long as we keep going

No shame about asking for help in waiting on the Lord
Who will renew our strength regardless of Whose we use
The only shame would be refusing His ride on Eagle Wings

The Journey of finding it's not brokenness we need not fear
When looking at our already broken reflection, it's knowing
Only way for healing to begin, is walking through the pain

We can kick, scream Jesus get the healing over with today
Or ask for His Comfort, His peace while waiting on Him in faith
Knowing His timing never failed doing one Miracle

When finally through to the other side of healing pain Will look back to
see all the fuss was over a scratch One little scar will not ruin God's
perfection in you

The Start to Find New Answer:

Part Three
Time For Rewards

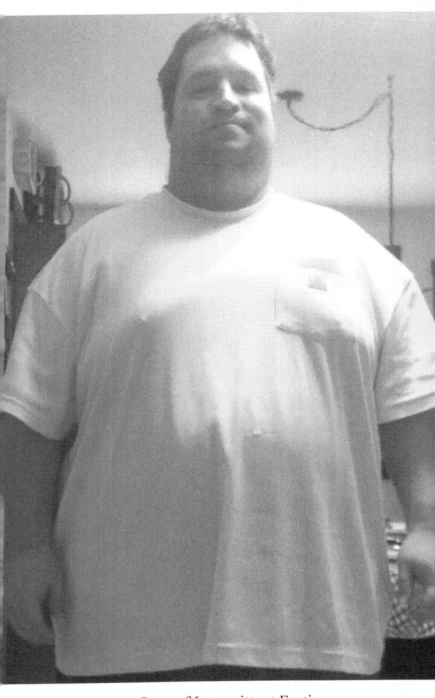

Start of Intermittent Fasting

CHAPTER THIRTY
Love Poetry

NOVEMBER OF 2016 I was asked by my cousin Roxanne to write her wedding poem for her wedding day May 21st of 2017. Well I write best in the moment thinking fresh and wrote her poem same day as I was asked. But in writing the poem it reopened the idea of doing a book with Love poetry, which I had started before Rainbows Hidden Treasures. Even though my first book was dedicated to the first online girl I fell I love with. But more on that further down.

Just because I was stuck at home, unable to drive, not really comfortable going to social events doesn't mean I wasn't looking for a girl I could fall in love with. I've asked a girl out twice, but got rejected both times. Getting Babiesa and stuttering doesn't boost the confidence much after that. I never talked to anyone because of fear of being made fun of. Call me sensitive to certain subjects; talking about girls was one of them. Though I struggled to build up courage to talk to girls in public. I still was feeling loneliness, a longing to know what it felt like to be loved. I have no problem talking to girls online, not worrying about getting words out without stuttering or my legs tightening from standing in one place too long.

Treating girls right was one of my principles to live by: #1 Living for God, #2 No alcohol, no drugs, no smoking. I wasn't going to let my gift of poetry get away from me, which meant keeping a sound mind and I didn't want to get tempted to like beer, didn't like seeing people get drunk and didn't want to be one of them, #3 Honesty, #4 Treat girls with respect.

I look for beauty inside out, like God's work of Living art. I love pretty smiles, and looked for girls online from dating sites, to online poker room. Though I stuck with Christian dating sites, I was mostly heartbroken with them.

I would talk with one for a while, write a few love poems, and then find out how fake she was. How I learned to spot scammers so good. I met a few that weren't fake, including one that I talked to up until my Grandma passed. Guess one of the reasons I didn't take it so hard was because I had an online girl I was talking to on the phone, but then shortly after I never heard from her again.

The next girl turned out to be crazy, and wanted me to go to India with her. One girl wanted me to get healthy first, after I told her my story. Up until then, I've only talked to a few that meant more than getting something I couldn't give.

I had an online friend on a Christian forum that I talked to, who was living with contentment of being single. So after getting tired of my heart getting broken despite writing 53 poems during those times. I just decided to learn to live being content being single with the window of God bringing me the one.

So after writing my cousin's wedding poem I got to work writing my new book, *Love Intertwined*, and God started teaching me more about His Love, and the love in marriage.

Roses Of Their Hearts

Out of dust came Adam, then with his rib, first love was born in Eve
God kissed their hearts with love knowing they needed each other
Witnessed by all of heaven's angels God's first wedding ceremony

God's all about love including the love between husband and wife
Those that trust Him with this love will find the souls of their love
Forget the world's compatible way to find love and stick to God's

Before we're born God has the perfect love to meet us at the crossroads
After all He knows us best, He kissed us with His love for love of hearts
With all of heaven blushing like the sunset sky God's rose waits for you

God planted roses inside Greg's heart while he was putting shoes on feet
That wasn't just feet he smelled, but the roses of love growing inside
Through the feeding of humility, waiting on the perfect moment to bloom

Hardships of the heart are the mulch God uses to prepare for His true love
Our impatience will be God's perfection to His teaching on works of love
Without forgiveness in the heart our love won't remain true

God planted roses inside Roxanne's heart while she thawed food for living
That wasn't the food melting, but the roses of love being fed, growing inside
Through the feeding of humanity, waiting on the perfect moment to bloom

Moment of truth came finding Greg and Roxanne standing in the crossroads

Roses of their hearts bloomed together, forever intertwined promises of
I do
God will always be with you, so lean on Him to provide the happily ever
after

Witnessed here today with all of Heaven's Angels and father of the
bride
Who give them away, with the groom standing before this wedding
ceremony?
As He marries Greg and Roxanne before the arch of His rainbow of
love

Now the tears of joy of those gone before us can be felt as never left
Because with Christ they're all here to celebrate this special wedding
Like the First wedding God performed for His Glory to be seen

CHAPTER THIRTY ONE
Not Alone

I DON'T KNOW if ever being on a date live and in person is written on the cards in God's plans for me, but that's okay. I am learning to trust God with His Will for me every day. The trials have been painful, but I also have learned of their joy, like it talks about in James 1.

Glass House

Along a country road there was this glass house in shape of a heart
The smudges with dirt makes it hard to notice and not nice to look at
Except for the light shining through the broken glass

If you stopped to look at this glass house in shape of a heart
You would see there was something about the holes in the glass
That they were broken from inside out

When looking through the holes in the glass house in shape of a heart
We will see that this heart made of glass is alive beating slowly up and down
Then without warning tremors start as if crying and more glass starts to break

Can't help but ask this glass house in shape of a heart why the tears of sorrow
Tremors started to stop a voice with sniffles, cries out you wouldn't understand
But, then again who can understand a broken heart that lost their love

Maybe someone that's been there, that's gone through a broken heart of love
What if there was another glass house in shape of a heart that was broken
This house in shape of a heart was not only broken but fixed because of love

The glass house in shape of a heart started crying again saying please fix me
I want to love again with true love that will never break again but always shine
With tears washed away broken glass swept away, the broken heart was fixed

Along a country road there's this glass house in shape of a heart
This house reflects the Son light off the windows made of crystals
If we stop and look close will see the broken made new of rainbows
Broken Hearts

Where would we be if the heartbroken refused to share their story?
Do we really think only heart to be broken is our own, are we that naïve?
We're not the first heart to be broken nor will we be the last

The Bible is full of broken hearts, failures and disappointments
But where would we be without them persevering through the storm?
How would we learn from their successes without seeing the journey?

Where would we be if those that failed stopped trying to overcome?
Do we really think we're the only ones that failed in dreams or goals?
We're not the first to fall on our faces or will we be the last

The Bible is full of broken hearts, failures, and disappointments
But where would we be if they refused to share how to overcome?
What if nobody wanted to share through his or her humility?

Where would we be if the disappointed just gave up without trying again?
Do we really think we're the only ones to be disappointed on life's turnouts?
We're not the first nor the last, not getting what we wanted only to be told no

The Bible is full of broken hearts, failures, and disappointments

But where would we be if they refused to share how Jesus came?
When Jesus appeared in the fire or walked on water, or died on a cross

How can writers be inspired to write when there's no inspiration shared?
Overcoming broken hearts, succeeding after failing a hundred times over
How small would the Bible be if nobody told how Jesus saved him or her?

Stories of broken hearts healing, past failures overcome by success
This is how God chose to write His letter of love because He knew
Hearts would be broken again, showed time and time again

The Bible is full of broken hearts, failures, and disappointments
But it's also full of love healing hearts, love lifting up the fallen
How big heaven will be with people that overcame life with love

I grew up being told fat was bad for you, like the fat in milk. So skim milk it was for most of my life. Even though I never liked the taste of skim, fat free milk. I just got lost in the sugar, high carb cereal I poured the milk on.

It was the same way of thinking towards yogurt, cheese, ice cream, but ice cream is loaded with sugar anyway. Diet soda was something else I grew up on, but turns out diet is really no better than regular, because the body reacts the same to sugar and artificial sweeteners. They raise insulin because of the glycemic making too much sugar.

Lean meats, high protein, taking the skin off the chicken to make it (you got it) less fattening. Turns out learning everything I knew about food was backwards. Low fat diets, low calories isn't the way to go.

Truth be told, it's the exact opposite of how our bodies were made, formed by God our Creator. What I should have been doing was cutting out the sugar and not the fat. I should definitely have cut out the sodas all together a long time ago.

Somewhere down the line of history, we started sacrificing quality for quantity. Then we started sacrificing quality of life, for the convenient way of life. We started using profit to sustain hunger instead of squashing it, and, in doing so, started losing the bigger picture for health.

Face it, the death we used to face – besides gunshots or other types of violence in the name of fear, envy, greed, and jealousy – was accidental. Sure, there might have been some diseases from lack of nutrients, because of actually having to hunt for your own food, actually putting in the work to grow the food.

But still, it wasn't highly processed like today, or, for that matter, highly modified in the name of greed and convenience. Sure, maybe at the start, it was done to save time from having to work all day, from hunting all day, traveling all day, instead of being at home with family.

Well, how has that really been working? Last I checked, we are still traveling, working all day for as many American dollars as we possibly can get, while we still spend less time at home with the family, and more importantly with God and His Holy Word.

Somewhere down the line in history we started to use the sugar we had, seldom using the five pound sack, trying to last the whole month, or until the next time we hitched the wagon to travel so long into town.

But as times grew easier – with inventions to get to town

faster to get more sugar – the demand for satisfying the sweet tooth started turning into greed for profit, instead of being satisfied with what we had.

That's the problem. When we look into the world instead of into the Word of God, we're never satisfied, wanting more and more, until we realize we can sell for something more valuable; except money still cannot buy happiness and true contentment in satisfaction.

Except with the sugar companies the greed continued over quality for their convenience, even though they knew by then sugar wasn't good. They didn't want to be disproven, however, so they set up the bad labels for fat and cholesterol.

So fast-forward to today. We're living on highly processed foods full of hidden carbs and sugars, which most Americans buy out of convenience instead of quality. Somewhere in history we decided to save time from cooking to have more family time at the table until it's time to leave again for the fast-paced way of life.

So how is that working for us? With our smartphones on, with our ears glued to the TV while eating fast food of sugar and protein and no real vegetables. Then when it comes to getting our health back, once again we're after convenience over quality, demanding that our health emerge from a magic pill instead of a magic seed that grew vegetables to sustain the health we lost in the name of convenience.

Companies took advantage of the demand to be fixed by pills, drug and paid into the healthcare system. At the same time, dieting companies took advantage of our obesity poor health, getting us to workout like crazy, while still blaming the fat we feared was making us more over weight. Once again convenience was winning over quality.

When are we going to do real studies on the toxicity of sugar on our bodies and how it's even worse combined with protein? Instead of lying about the facts found in the health benefits of fat that fed off grass, and other green vegetation, and lying about the cholesterol in eggs.

If cholesterol was so bad why does our bodies make so much, and why is our brain made of fat if it was so bad, and why weren't we told we need fat to repair fatty tissue, and why aren't we told cholesterol is needed to repair blood vessels damaged by sugar?

We consume way too much every day, instead of sparingly, like we used to before we gave into living for convenience instead of the quality way of life and living in daily the Word of God.

Yes, I know it sounds like I'm speaking of conspiracies, except I'm living proof and I'm not sharing my thoughts, my beliefs to make more money. I'm sharing my story of what I've gone through and found out, what makes sense to me and create more awareness based on what's finally worked for me, after a very long hard road of finding truth about what was going on inside my body.

I mean, I was living the convenient way of life, falling for the misunderstanding about the truth of what feeds our bodies. The low fat way of eating while consuming high quantities of carbs and protein, not to mention gmo foods that cause insulin resistance; it was no wonder I developed deficiencies, body issues, and weakness.

Getting Babiesa and going undiagnosed for 24 years made matters worse before my cousin, a Microbiologist and an expert in tick diseases, discovered what the doctors in Pennsylvania failed to do.

They can argue against me all they want with their outdated understanding. I witnessed first hand what was in my blood test. Since the discovery that the blood test revealed, I have been listening to my gut feelings and using my faith in Christ Jesus, accepting the fact that I was on my own in discovering how to get my body healthy and in shape again.

Thankfully, God showed me I really wasn't all alone, as He showed me the way to people that knew the Truth, that would educate me about what was really going on inside my body, and on why I wasn't getting the nutrients needed.

I wasn't losing weight and keeping it off, no matter how I tried keeping the calorie intake down, no matter how little fat I consumed, how long I was able to last on the treadmill, which varied day by day.

I wasn't keeping my blood sugars down, wasn't sleeping right, until I gave Dr. Berg's intermittent fasting and ketosis plan a try. Then everything I knew before went out the window with the rest of the garbage that I was told was to get me healthy yet did the exact opposite.

And so I started doing the exact opposite of what I knew, and started feeling my body begin to heal at last. I did have to sort through mixed emotions.

I know I can't really blame anyone, and I'm not really trying to. Like I said before, I'm just trying to create the awareness to be more educated about what we consume, and about what we shouldn't consume just because it's convenient.

Face it, when the dust settles and it becomes clear, no matter how big the cover up, we've all lost our ways. Not only in the way of living according to God's Word, but also in the way of how we're Created to eat.

We started living to eat and drink what we wanted for pleasure, instead of eating, drinking to live with the occasional pleasures of life. Once again we started going after the forbidden fruit, (which, by the way, was never said in God's Word to be an apple).

Since the birth of sin we've been saying no to the way God provides, giving into the lust of our eyes, and loading up on gluttony.

When will we repent of our sinful ways, and get back to the way of Truth through grace and humility of what Jesus has done for us in order to make us healthy and holy.

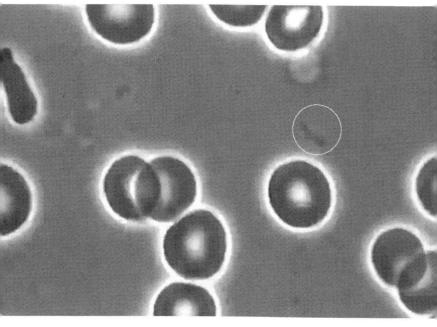

Babiesa Parasite

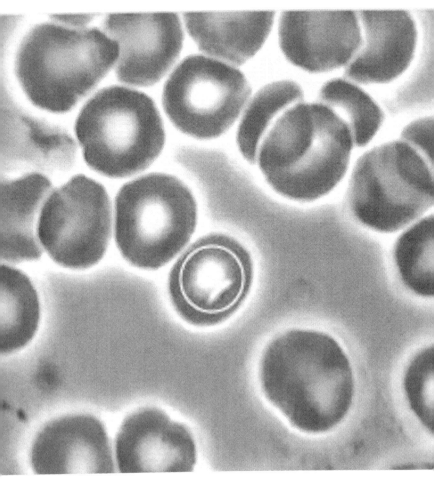

Babiesa Parasite

CHAPTER THIRTY TWO
Broken Enough

THROUGH PAIN, THROUGH my own broken down body I got to know the faithfulness of the Lord Jesus Christ. Even though I'm not perfect, and should have spent way more time trying than I have. Instead of playing games, watching TV, but still the Lord is faithful.

I am glad I was given a voice to pray over the broken in the Social media world, like Facebook, Twitter. Even though I don't post unless I have something enlightening to say, but I do pray whether they ask for it or not.

Truth is, we're all broken in some shape or form, just not always broken enough until we feel the painful truth of what we've been missing. Busyness of the world through narrow visions leaves us missing a lot. Thankfully, God has ways to get our attention. Not as punishment, but wake up calls, warning signs of stop, dead end ahead, bridge out.

Psalm 91, Psalm 139, the book of James is what I read when feeling lost, broken, confused, afraid. But the Lord is, always faithful. He's there to lend a hand when we ask and puts us back together when we use the faith given to believe enough to take action.

8/14/2012
Faithful

Some scientists say the world is billions of years old
Only God knows for sure, the number doesn't matter
But what does, is that He is faithful to those He loves

Millions into billions people have walked this earth since day six
Then the first sin came marking us all for death until Jesus came
God the so Faithful in love, gave His only Son to die for us

From the persecuted, to the sinners though forgiven, one out of one
Death still takes us even though it's been defeated through resurrection
Just no longer matters, when Jesus takes us home it's just a corpse

Millions into billions, past, present, future people have walked this earth
One by one, we live till Jesus says come home good and faithful
servant
God the so Faithful keeps His promise of never leaving

Those that have tried to stop us from being faithful to the living Truth
They failed to see He that has gone before us gave victory in their
defeat
Even though they refused to believe, God is faithful to those that do

From day one, to the end the number in heaven is too many to count
Those that lived a short life, to those that lived a long one they served
The impact made is more than anybody but God knows

Look up in the millions into billions of stars to see the light of the
faithful
One by one we have taken our place to shine beside the Father in
heaven

God the so Faithful in love, John 3:16 will be understood eternity is
forever

CHAPTER THIRTY THREE
Trust

WE DON'T HAVE to fear being broken. I've been afraid of being out in the dark, in the night, in the woods. I've had fear go through me just walking down the driveway.

But the truth is, I had nothing to fear; something wasn't coming out to get me, because Jesus is always there. Unfortunately, our trust isn't always there with our faith because we still fear to be broken, as if our bodies were made of eggshells.

Take the story of Humpty Dumpty read or read to as children. Humpty sat on the wall with a shell easily broken by a fall. How easily we could be Humpty Dumpty, easy to be offended, easy to strike back at the slightest touch, afraid to be knocked down, afraid to be broken.

For whatever reason, we have a hard time trusting Jesus to be there, to catch us when we fall. Truth is, Jesus has always been there, we've just been struggling, wiggling too much, not holding still, falling out of His grasp.

What we don't realize while we're cursing, yelling at Him, asking where He was. Jesus is picking up our brokenness and putting us back together, giving us a harder shell.

7/2/2013
Humpty Dumpty

Humpty Dumpty sat on the wall staring back at me
So I thought until I recognize the reflection in the mirror
Then I fell down weeping at my brokenness

So many of us walk around thinking I'm ok the way I am
Not realizing we're walking on our own cracked eggshells
Before seeking help need to swallow the pride that pushed us

Jesus is the Messiah that will put broken pieces back together
By the power of His cross, His blood is the glue that fixes us again
His forgiveness has made us clean and has made us new

Humpty Dumpty sat on the wall again still staring back at me
Thought I was made like new again when Jesus came into me
But I am falling down again broken

So many of us walk around thinking just because I call myself Christian
That I'll never be broken, feel pain again, that life will be all riches and
glory
Not realizing the world would break us because of His glory

Jesus keeps fixing us His blood never runs dry, but we still keep
walking Before He's finished never realizing we're missing pieces until
we fall down again
Our pride keeps pushing us towards the edge until we fall

Humpty Dumpty sat on the wall, but this time when I fell broken
Asked Jesus to take my pride in total surrender while on my knees
We became whole, no longer fragile, but strong like a rock, like Jesus

7/9/2012
His Pain, His Body

Why does God allow good men to get sick in a vegetable state?
Why did God allow Lazarus to die only to be raised four days later?
Because sometimes it takes being broken down to nothing

Sometimes Jesus hurts too His pain travels down through the body
Yet we don't always feel His pain because sin still runs underneath
Leaving us paralyzed to feel His tears running down our face

We're the body Jesus uses to reach out, helping those that need hope
But sometimes His body doesn't respond so must break us down to see
That someone needs Him and it's now they need to see He cares

Why does God allow little children to be born only to die young?
Why did God allow a sick girl to die in her sleep only to be awakened?
Because we're all miracles waiting to be awakened from our slumbers

Sometimes Jesus hurts too His pain travels through our body
Yet we don't realize it's His pain we're feeling in our anger state
The tears running aren't ours but His as we forget He weeps too

We're the body Jesus uses to reach out wanting to perform miracles
But sometimes His body falls asleep needing awakened by any means
So that His healing hands will be seen being placed in the people that hurt

Why does God allow evil to run wild in the hearts that were good?
Well why did we choose to bite into that forbidden fruit having it all?
Because satan planted the seed of jealousy wanting more

Jesus hurts too His pain travels through His Children
Through His stripes we're healed but leaves us scars
So that His broken body will be seen being restored

CHAPTER THIRTY FOUR
Constant

VISIONS OF WRITING my poems over the years, no matter how many I've written. One message has stayed constant even as the outline changed poem to poem.

The Message has always been the center point of the Gospel of Jesus Christ. Even when writing love poems, about inspirational people, the Gospel in some way or another is laid out to see we need Jesus to make things work.

The Gospel doesn't just come out of people dressed in fancy suits, people that dress to be perfect, with perfect bodies. Take the Carriers of the Gospel in the Bible, who were fishermen, tax collectors, a virgin teenager, some kings, but not many.

Some were former persecutors of Christ Followers. Jesus can and will use anything, anyone to carry His Gospel.

Humility is the greatest quality of a Carrier of the Gospel of Jesus Christ.

I am thankful to Jesus for letting me be one of those who shares His Gospel.

6/9/2012
His Gospel

Sometimes He rides in on a Harley dressed in leather
With a few tattoos that tells a story of the past he lived
Now rides on High living proof, He lives through our mistakes

People judged by the shirts on their backs not seen for the Truth
The self-righteous often miss by proclaiming one gospel, one way
Not realizing they preach to Jesus Himself

Sometimes He's in a dress walking in high heels, hoping to be loved
With a few broken hearts, HIV running in the veins tells her storied past
Now she sings on high of His living grace, proof He lives in mistakes

People judged without a second thought by the life they lived
The self-righteous don't see the changes with their one gospel
Not realizing it's Jesus Himself walking

There may be one gospel but it's expressed in many different ways
By the many different people through ways only Jesus can explain
But expressed through His love proof that He lives through our
mistakes

Sometimes He's in a wrap holding a spear in the jungles of Africa
With a bone through his nose that tells a story of how his people lived
Now He preaches on high how Jesus through a missionary saved him

Jesus hears His people cry out that they're ready to be saved by
anybody
So He moves with His body in anybody that's willing to serve Him now
Doesn't care how they're dressed as His love works in mysterious
ways
People will be saved by the little bit of heaven shown inside the shirts
The hands of Jesus will soften the hardest heart, heal the brokenness
Jesus died so that we can live through our mistakes in His gospel

CHAPTER THIRTY FIVE
Stories Behind The Poems

HOPING THE STORIES behind the poems haven't been too depressing, but it's my life before and after poems written. Sometimes I wonder what it'd be like to be a little normal to others. But so far dealing with mysteries has been my normal way of living.

Don't know why I've had to deal with a broken down body that no doctor has had a clue how to fix. Don't know why I can't do much physically up until this point of my life. Dealing with questions of why can't you drive, and only giving what sounds like excuses without living life in my shoes is hard.

There are a lot of things I wish I was able to do, but can't because of limitations and fear.

But I've learned to adjust and lived with an open mind, while trying to trust the Lord Jesus my Savior, the best I can. I am so thankful for simple pleasures like golfing when I can, listening to music, and talking to friends online. Because of living at home, not able to go anywhere, I've been able to meet people all over the world, mostly the states. I've helped as a listener to people, how much of a help, only they can say.

God has His reasons for me being an online missionary,

and for giving me the gift of visions and poetry. Even though I may never know why the three-line format is a must for me, or why my mind can't think due to noise sensitivity, or why I have to do things a certain way to keep stress down, I wouldn't adjust a thing.

I will be eternally grateful for the way God has chosen to use me. And, again, I wouldn't change anything that's happened in my life.

We're all made differently, given different lives to live for the different purposes of God. The Truth is, everyone sees things differently even though similarities are present in our stories, and these connections make the inspirational difference, to keep us going, to never lose the hope of living better.

2/25/2011
What Is Real

Shining of the moon over the ocean natures own lighthouse
A great horned owl flies down, closing in to capture a mouse
Mysteries captured on canvas, masterpieces of the night

So what is real to you animation on paper or a real life living canvas?
Accidents of mother nature reformed or created to perform in praises
One is living the life they're created to be but are we real or just a canvas

Sun shining sparkles through the raindrops creating radiance of color
Deer running through a meadow as if heading for the end of the rainbow
Mysteries captured on canvas or masterpiece of the sun kissing rain

So what is real to you pictures worth thousand words or living life
Worth ten times more than any camera can capture to relive the tale

One is being still in the picture, the other is moving while time freezes

Mountains that are steep yet mountain sheep run as no fear holds them
Rams clash heads echoing that sounds like thunder breaking sound barriers
Mysteries unheard like trees falling in the forest or a masterpiece that all hear

What is real to you? Let there be no mistake the Creator made no animation
There's no canvas being painted with all of creation standing still waiting to see
God is the Creator and we're the living masterpiece given honor to praise Him

Do we let the rocks cry out in the mystery of why we don't see the living truth?
What is real to the Heavenly Father is the Love that was Breathed over Creation
Only mystery is why it takes so long for our eyes to see what we should believe

Can't Be The Same

We can't all be living the same dream, it's how they break
Got to stop making others live your dreams by your values
We got to realize we're not designed to be equal

No matter how many want to play 1st base not everyone can
Someone has to pitch, catch, play like a team to make last out
Can't live life where everyone has the same job

Male and female that's how God formed us to be, the way to live
Even though we breathe the same, heart beats the same, we're not
We're designed to be different, to lift each other up, raise His Family

Being the hands of Christ is good, but how would we get there
Unless learned to do handstands all the time, but then how would
We lend a Christ-like hand to others? If our hands are busy?

Someone needs to be humble enough to be the feet of Jesus
Take us where He wants us to go, need a humble heart to match

The face that says Jesus loves you

Life's not about equality, not about who gets the most money
We're not all right, but half left, until we get this, will be left behind
If we're not willing to work together, to work different parts of the body

Until Jesus comes back through the clouds, we the love of Jesus
We're to be the body of Christ, working together as One for Him
Because He died to save us, and we can't live for Him falling apart

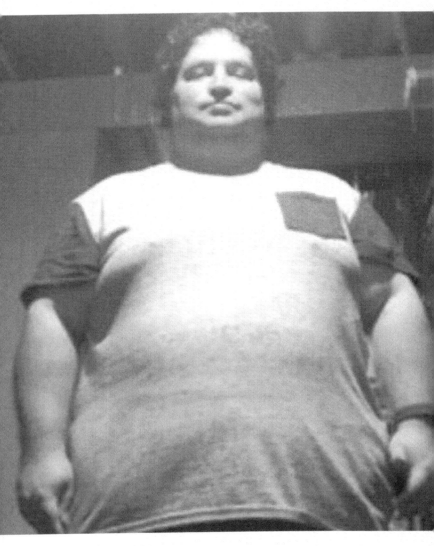

2 Months Into Finding Answers

CHAPTER THIRTY SIX
Well Equipped

ONE OF THE things I love about my gift of poetry is never really knowing who it's for. It could be for me, yet at times, when shared on Facebook, I've seen replies of "I needed that today". This is enough, if I only had one reason for sharing a poem. Nobody knows except God who and when someone needs to hear the message.

I may never sell many books because of this, and truth be told, it does get frustrating. But when in the right mind, I realize it's about ministering to others, and that here resides true success. My joy comes from the smiles on faces when I give them a book. The smiles are the reward of a job well done. Maybe one day, I will get different rewards, but God provides when the needs arise.

There isn't one who was created unequipped to do what he or she was meant to do. God is a God of love, but also a God of all the details. There's no crack, no corner that God missed with His paintbrush.

Even at the moment of the first foolish thought of sin in the Garden of Eden, He had the plan to fix everything, not only in place, but also in motion. Chance after chance was given until Jesus took off His Crown to be born, first in the witness of animals, until the Wisemen and Shepherds could get there.

But He was born to die for our sins. Our every mistake that came to thought was forgiven at the Cross and God's plan of fixing everything was completed when the stone was rolled away and Jesus sat back up. What a feeling it is to be forgiven and to have the weight of the world taken off the shoulders!

Truth be told (By the way, my favorite saying of Jesus's): Nothing is about us, it's nothing that has to do with this world. Everything has to do with loving God through a relationship in Jesus Christ. God created man (us) to be with us, so that we could love Him freely with our will, of our own choosing.

Sure sounds foolish to those still lost, not understanding that they still wander in the dark. But for those that have found the Light of Jesus, there's no place we'd rather be, and/or doing than resting with Jesus in the Presence of our Heavenly Father.

Miracle Shoulders

Sometimes the world seems flat even though it's round
The weight of the world is on my shoulders and I'm falling
With the sky crashing down around me, need a miracle now

We're not created to hold the world in place to do its bidding
That's not why God our Father breathed Life into dusty bones
So give Him the world and let Him give you Peace

Life's not fair in this world we get born into for years unknown
Satan tries to get us to believe, so we're distracted from Truth
More we carry of the world forced onto our shoulders the better

When we carry so much of the world flat on our back can't see
Satan's foot sticking out to trip us over the edge of our reality
Doesn't want us to see God's hand reaching for our burdens

We're not Created to carry the world's burdens, but to Love
Why Jesus the Son of God was born on Christmas Morning
So He could take our Burdens to the cross on His shoulders

Might feel like we're falling over the edge of a flat world
But Jesus will be there to catch you, to remind you it's Ok
The Miracle will always be there for you to take hold

Let the burdens go to the cross of Jesus and He will give
The desires of the heart that you're longing for of peace
Life will still have ups and downs, but you're in His Hands

John 14:27

Goodbye To Burdens

Nobody knows how to say goodbye to his or her burdens
Not anymore, we try to hang on when we should let go
No wonder we're so red in the face sweating hate

Things done to us, let's do unto them until blood spills
Eye for an eye, tooth for a tooth misquoted time again
If only we had enough Faith to Forgive

Justice will be done, when we've forgiven the wrong
The healing of injustice will begin not for their sake
But for our sake, so we don't keep hurting ourselves

God sees what they've done to you, and to His only Son
Who not only died for your sins, But also for theirs, every one's
We do unto them, as we do unto Jesus to forgive at the cross

Nobody knows how to say goodbye to burdens until we read
Where Jesus says goodbye to them for us when He forgives
Don't need to wave, just forgive to say Goodbye, Hello Jesus

Mistaken Forgiven

We're only human, no matter who we are, what we do
We're living with daily mistakes, day after day, the difference
The only difference is that we've been forgiven

Forgiven even though we have yet to understand, Jesus said
That's what Jesus said while dying for us on the cross before
We fully understood it was our sin He was dying for, not His

Mistakes started with Adam and Eve, passed on to generations
Through every child born, they're born a sinner walking in darkness
Until introduced to the Light of Jesus, who forgave us in the dark

We're headed for the same destination, even though all different
Traveling on the same road just at different times, like day and night
Don't always hear or see the same message, on the same passed sign

Forgiven that's what we were before, we understood it's what Jesus said
Why can't we forgive those that don't quite understand what they say too?
Doesn't matter if it was said in silence or in action, they're to be forgiven

There was a house with two children in two different levels of the house
The Father cried out to them a message of love for both to hear, but only
Was only one of the children that understood, the closest one to him

We're only human, making mistakes daily, what we're born to do
Until we're reborn through Jesus Christ, surrendering to Him daily
But there's no mistaking we've been forgiven on the cross

CHAPTER THIRTY SEVEN
Release

WE MAY NEVER find the Answers to life's tragedies, at least not the ones we want to hear. I know my darkest days were when I lost my Grandfather. Even though I knew He was with Jesus no better place to be, still hurt like hell.

But to tell you the Truth, this world is not our home. We should be grateful for time spent with those we love, let go the bitterness, hate, and anger, and release the thoughts of why it happened to me. Being victims of sin, theirs or ours, in the coldness of reality isn't about me. Instead, it's about overcoming everything that the king of darkness throws at us in this world before sitting next to Jesus Christ.

I wish to God nobody had to go through, live with somebody else's madness in his or her small, only me world where he or she treats others like their personal puppets.

The good news is we're never walking, riding in this world alone. Jesus is with us, every step, every turn, every crossroad of life. There's not one storm we've gone through that Jesus hasn't gone through with us. Staying mad at someone else's mad world, blaming God is only hurting ourselves and wasting our time, going in circles until we let

Jesus lead us again. We have to get out of the boat and walk on the water at some point in our broken down life of a boat. The mustard seed of faith grows in all of us, waiting for us to take root and grow stronger with every obstacle overcome.

Backwards Of James

When are we going to stop threatening to take our ball home?
Every time something is said or done which we don't see to eye
Here we've grown from spoiled kids to grumpy old men

How are we going to show the Love of Jesus when we
Don't remember the Love Jesus shown to us on our walk
How He listened to the whine from our voices in complaints

Quick to boycott, quick to protest instead of wrapping our arms
Around those that just want to be heard in the chaos and confusion
Slow we're to remember what it was to be lost, wandering in the dark

How long has it been since we've been saved, if we've ever been at all?
The way we've unpacked our bags settling in with what we knew of God
Instead of going on the Journey of growing in the Lord's footsteps

Backwards of James we've gotten quick to speak slow to listen
Our anger is a runaway horse losing the bit to control, a match
Forgotten among the ashes of the forest fire of our lives

For the Love of Jesus give back the ball, get back to Amazing Grace
The errors of our ways have been forgiven, no longer a wretch lost
But now been saved, and being called to act like the Children of God

Guilt Feels Forgiven

I know the first reaction to wrong is to get mad, but
Before getting even get over yourself and think of others
Last thing anyone wants to do is make mistakes

Nobody feels guiltier than the one who's done the act
Unless demons are inside, but still does nothing good to
Raise the Voice, till the whole world hears the revenge

Accidents will happen, we're only human in need of saving grace
Just one off balance moment will lead us off target into hooking left
But all a golfer wants to do is hit the ball straight in life or on the course

Last thing we want to do is feel guilty inside with angry voices in our heads
That's not including the one wronged, only way to move on is forgiveness
This is how the fire gets put out and healing of burns begins

Don't go to social media right after being wronged and go to lynching
That's not of Jesus who said to forgive 70x7, because He knows the heart
And He knows the wrong will be made right when the guilt feels forgiven

Thrive Without Hurt

Everyone wants to thrive, just not going through circumstances
That leads to finding what it takes for us to thrive in this world
Just as long we don't have to go through the pain to thrive

But we really have to go through the pain in order to find what it takes
What it really means, to what it looks like to thrive instead of struggle
Without the pain we can't build the Character to Thrive

If only we lived in a world where we didn't have to find Answers
Connected to questions we don't understand, and can't move
Until we have the logic to those Answers we seek to thrive

But we really have to go through trusting the Answer without logic
That gives us the understanding to why we're going through hell
When we just want to be left alone living our on life for me

Everyone wants to thrive without the benefit of the doubt from you
About the Truth of needing to love each other, with Love from God
We don't want to hear, in order to thrive we need the heart break

But we really have to go through betrayal, the stabbing in the back
So we can truly learn how to forgive, even though it hurts like hell
Because Jesus went through hell to forgive, to save us of our sins

Learning to Love, to forgive no matter the hurt we go through in life
Because face it, falling off the world's peddle stool without Jesus hurts
But knowing we got forever living with Jesus will have us thriving together

Devastating News, But Jesus

Devastating news on a blue-sky day takes the breath away
That leaves questions; of what do we do now after the shock?
First breathe Jesus in thanks, then breathe out Jesus who Knows

Answers to life's hardest questions are found in Jesus Son of God
Who knows first hand what we're going through, living among us
After being born over 2,000 years ago to walk beside, talk to us

Devastating news makes God weep too when He takes them Home
Doesn't want us to feel Heaven's gain as our pain to bear after grieving
But instead rejoice even when shedding tears, knowing not alone
Jesus is with us always, even when we can't feel His Presence
Trust Him to waken in time of need when we call, even in weakness
Our faith will be enough to hang on to His promises

Death isn't the end, but an open door with hand of Jesus reaching
Life that's everlasting, free from pain, only land of joy awaits them
Burdens are left going through and given a crown coming out

Devastating news comes with gray clouds, but Jesus is the Son
That breathes back in the reminder He's got everything controlled
Let the Joy of the Lord be the Sun and the Moon that shines through

CHAPTER THIRTY EIGHT
Healing

WHILE I MAY never know what was keeping my body from working normally, I have my theories. Doctors have theirs. I also know what I've seen with my own eyes. I just don't know exactly when Babiesa parasites invaded my body.

I also know I am healing and will continue to heal until Jesus makes me whole again. Until then, and while I am still healing, my stories and poems continue taking a new birth, growing stronger, deeper. I don't need my every mystery to be solved.

I just need to keep trusting that Jesus is leading me to where I belong, and to where I am needed to write and keep sharing my stories and poems. Because He knows who needs to hear them next for their lives to change around. So they too can stop trying to solve every mystery that's happened to them.

Just live the life Jesus has given you to live with no regrets. See the trials for what they really are, not trials of sorrow, but of joy, knowing your faith is getting stronger, and that your perseverance will last until Jesus takes you home to see those that have gone before you, Friends and Family, all

Children of God.

Until the biggest Family Reunion takes place I will keep writing in hopes someone will read and will be inspired to be the difference that someone else sees the Light of Jesus to be found out of the darkness.

Don't be afraid of perceptions, of being seen as broken. Truth be told, we're all broken. We just don't know it until we see the reflection of Jesus putting us back together, one broken piece at a time. The pain we feel isn't from being broken, but from being set, bones, heart and flesh being put back in place. When we start itching to be home, then we know we're close to having our healing completed.

Scratch that itch with praises of thanks to Jesus for putting up with our groaning, whining, overreacting in anger instead of thanks. Jesus loves us and it shouldn't be a mystery any longer, just accepted and love back the best we know how. We're no mystery to Jesus, and Jesus is not a mystery to solve, just a Loving Savior who is the King Of Kings to be accepted as our Friend.

Don't Be

Don't be afraid to be seen in person, live for all to see
Don't be ashamed of the way God is building character
The past is gone, the only thing remains is learned

The only flaws are what we make, not what others think
If we truly believe God is good and all He makes is flawless
Then let go the doubt about how He's making you

Everything that's happening to us, around us is for His good
Even what's to be made evil will be turned into good for Him

His Kingdom has no end, His goodness will never stop

No more looking in the mirror and walking away to forget
If Jesus is our Savior, then we have the Holy Spirit, hear Him
Let the Spirit be your mirror, remind the goodness bestowed

God uses our story of how He brought us back to saving grace
How there's nothing we can, can't do which His grace won't cover
Through His grace we're redeemed, through His love we're held

Newborn Kicks of Love

Father's eyes, Mamma's cheekbones with a heart for God
She will be born with the gift of seeing through Love's eyes
But won't know it until shown the way to know Him

Reflection of the Father, perspective received from the Mother
Words rained down feeds the growth of what sprouts of action
That gives the belief they're who God made them to be

All of this starts the moment of conception when God breathed
Life in the Mother's womb, forming little heartbeats of first thoughts
Getting to know the Parents and Heavenly Father until birth

Father's eagerness to run ahead to explore the unknown limitations
While the Mother will bring her back to reality with the voice of reason
The call of Love will always bring them back home

Correction of the Father, prayers unceasing by the Mother guide her
Through all the unknowns until the Light gets turned on in a dark world
Then the Holy Spirit will help make the Night Light brighter

All of the kicks felt are the communications of a whole new Love
coming
Prepare for everything and anything, but will still be overwhelmed in
awe
As you will learn every single word spoken before birth was heard

Let the Love for her be heard as she listens for your voice
Through the interpretation of God she will start to understand
There's another side to Love stored in the heart's mind at birth

Love Does

Love sees where we're going and what's in front of us
Love does what's needed to keep us heading straight
When everything is going wrong, can count on Love

How we get their remains on what wills we choose to use
How long to get there depends on how long we fight His Will
One thing we can count on is His Love doing what needs done

Love knows what we're fighting and knows the final results
Love does what's needed to keep us from losing our heads
Even if that means laying weapons down and having us repent

How much loss we feel depends on how long we keep fighting
Even in victories casualties can be high no matter why we fight
One thing we can count on is His Love doing what needs done

Love gets what we're going through, He's been through it all
Why Love came from Heaven to Earth to live among us, to know
What it was like to be loved, only to be betrayed, to pay for our Sins

Love will be soft when needs to, Love will be hard when needs to be
Love does what's needed to remind us we need to forgive, to be
forgiven
Just as Love forgave us when dying on the cross, before we even
understood

One thing we can count on is Love doing what needs done to be Holy
And we're Children of the most High God, our Father who wants us
Holy
Love does what's needed for us to act Holy because He Loves us so

Like Rain, Like Words

The Lord knows every raindrop that ever hit the ground
Like He knows the name of everyone that calls His Name
And every drop, every word reaches His ear

Doesn't matter if they're in a mist or a hurricane downpour
Every drop, every word produces the work they're meant to do

Which is to bring glory by feeding His Creation, hearing Children

The rain can leave devastation before returning to the atmosphere
But our words can also leave damage beyond that only He repairs
But unlike the rain our words can't be taken back once spoken

The Lord knows the lightning of our tongues produces thunder
The storms we create from gossip better left alone than to spark
The fire leaving relationships praying for rain to put them out

Humility will lead us to forgiveness when we repent in smolder
Being the rain God wants us to be that will heal the land to grow
Washing the blackness of our words away

The Lord knows every raindrop falling even in the middle of nowhere
Just like every voice that calls His name, no matter where they be He
Hears the voice of every single heartbeat, Knows who, where you are

CHAPTER THIRTY NINE
Food Adaptation

ADAPTING TO NEW ways of thinking about the right foods to eat can be hard unless desperate like me to lose weight and keep it off.

I mean I used to love eating burgers and fries, pizza, fried chicken. But after learning the truth of what I was consuming and what the combination did to raise a diabetic's insulin – like a roller coaster not to mention getting the blood sugars out of wack.

It was no wonder I was falling asleep two hours after what used to be my favorite foods. After being educated about the foods I was eating and the hidden ingredients, I started changing the way I looked at foods.

I started calling them for what they really were, crap. The American diet truly is made of synthetic fake crap that turns the digestion system all out of wack. For example, take the traditional thanksgiving, Christmas Day dinner. Which I now see as the protein (Turkey) three sugar sides (mashed potatoes, corn, stuffing) four if adding sweet potato with marshmallows, and no I don't count the green bean casserole as a vegetable because of not having any nutrients left after adding mushroom soup with hidden sugar (high fructose corn syrup) and already cooked up green beans.

I find it unfortunate now that I've learned the truth about the turkey and being unfairly blamed for making people on an insulin roller coaster sleepy. The combination of protein and sugar (carbohydrates) is very bad if you keep doing it over and over again. Not to mention about the GMO (genetically modified organisms) foods especially in corn and soy, this is how we develop diabetes if not born with it.

Not only adapting to the right foods, but knowing how to find them is the real challenge. Learning to read labels to spot hidden ingredients makes grocery shopping slow. So I started looking for foods without high fructose corn syrup, modified cornstarch (MSG) (Monosodium glutamate), Maltodextrin, anything high on the glycemic index and insulin index.

I tried my best to limit the condiments that had soy (triggers insulin resistance), which was very hard to do since I preferred creamy dressings like ranch over vinegar dressings, and also liked mayonnaise.

Thankfully, God gave me the joy of cooking with a creative sense of taste. So it didn't become difficult finding new favorite dishes. I've added a few recipes at the end of the book. I understand those that are afraid of losing their favorite pleasure foods, but as I quickly found out, we don't have to lose them. Just change the ingredients to the way they are made. Take out the bad ingredients, replace with good and safe ingredients.

There are low carb recipes for bread, cookies, cakes, pies.

Though being a diabetic at the start of intermittent fasting and ketosis I limited the thoughts of having these foods until I reached a weight loss goal point.

And if at some point I get stuck like I already have, then I start limiting those pleasure food thoughts again. New favorite foods will be found. Giving up soda wasn't that hard either, after learning the Truth, being educated about what I drink. Herbal teas, green tea, water with lemon or lime satisfies me.

Becoming educated, changing my thoughts, and the way I ate has led me to answers on how to heal my body. Specifically, and as it relates to my reader, I truly believe getting educated about what goes into our bodies, and, more importantly, knowing what should not go into our bodies, will be a better way for all to achieve good health than any medication.

CHAPTER FORTY
Answers

F OR THE LAST 17 to 20 years, I prayed for my weight to go down, and to stay down, because, each doctor's visit, the medical staff directed me to lose weight, said that what I was going through with Babiesa symptoms was because of my obesity. More recently, though, for the past seven years, I prayed to lose weight to get healthy, so I can do more physically.

My prayers were being answered through my health coach, even though before June 2017 she might not have asked me to join her intermittent fasting group if it meant losing my business.

It was in this group, while researching intermittent fasting, that God started revealing answers to my prayers through finding Dr. Eric Berg on YouTube. Becoming educated on the way my body works and how it needs to function has opened my eyes up to sugar and insulin resistance. I learned intermittent fasting and ketosis was the way to correct the problem.

I've been losing weight since, down from 319 lbs. to 274 lbs. and counting down. I'm hoping by the time this book is published, I will be below 250 lbs. My goal is to get down to

200 lbs. and then I will write a new book. Until then, I leave these final thoughts and poems.

Not only did I get a new insight on sugar and insulin resistance, but I also got a new insight on how sugar is like sin. How sin, when first committed, tastes sweet like sugar, and, with each sin afterward, satan keeps pouring in the sugar sin addictions. Getting us to blame everything else, coming up with every excuse to justify the committed sin.

That is, until we are awakened to the Truth that we need Jesus and we need redemption through repentance of our sins. The cross of Jesus offers forgiveness after we acknowledge the bitterness and the cost of our sin. Thank God that He sent His only Son to take away the bitter aftertaste of sin, and left behind His true, sweet-tasting Salvation.

Sugar and Sin

The forbidden fruit full of sugar and of sin, just because
We had to have it, lack of understanding didn't stop us
Ignorance what a poor excuse to the door of Consequence

Sugar and sin, toxic to the body and soul, yet blinded to both
Until are bellies are kings of the hill, fires of the soul going out
Insulin and God resistances give no winner, only death

Feeding addictions with more of the same never helps anyone
Hidden or in plain sight still affects the body and soul the same
Giving a diabetic sugar isn't a cure for hyperglycemic just a ride

The Lord made our bodies, our souls, No detail was a mistake
Was a perfect running machine, until we had to fix being perfect
Been running broken down ever since

Intermittent fasting and ketosis along with repentance is needed
Healing of the body, and of the soul, Jesus has given us the chance
Now it's up to us to accept and believe we have the faith to be saved

Don't Be

Don't be afraid to be seen in person, live for all to see
Don't be ashamed of the way God is building character
The past is gone, the only thing remains is learned

The only flaws are what we make, not what others think
If we truly believe God is good and all He makes is flawless
Then let go the doubt about how He's making you

Everything that's happening to us, around us is for His good
Even what's to be made evil will be turned into good for Him
His Kingdom has no end, His goodness will never stop

No more looking in the mirror and walking away to forget
If Jesus is our Savior, then we have the Holy Spirit, hear Him
Let the Spirit be your mirror, remind the goodness bestowed

God uses our story of how He brought us back to saving Grace
How there's nothing we can, can't do to which His Grace won't cover
Through His Grace we're redeemed, through His Love we're held

I hope eventually I will be healed enough and physically in shape to do more. Hopefully, I will be more in shape to travel alone and visit those online that have made an impact in my life. Maybe, I'll even get my driver's license and acquire a job, getting off disability income.

Until then, I will take one day at a time until I can get two workouts in a week, until I can add a third workout, and so on. Doing things right means taking longer.

The body can only burn two lbs. of fat per week and

that's if it is doing everything correctly, getting the right nutrients the body needs to work. Taking the time to get educated and not just accepting advice because someone told you differently, finding out where and how it was compiled, and who paid for the study. We get one body on earth that God made by His Design. You choose what goes in it, but make sure it goes along with the way God intended and that it's not modified to work against it.

Good intentions don't necessarily mean good results. We can't play and act like God, can only follow and trust Him to provide the very best. It doesn't get more perfect except from what comes from Him.

Don't be afraid to get broken, to feel broken, lost and confused. When we're weak, He is strong. When we're down to nothing, it means He's up to something. And even if it's satan starting something like he did with Job.

Don't be afraid. Don't stay angry. It's ok to question why, but don't stop praising and thanking the Lord, because what is used for evil and bad intentions will be turned into good.

Romans 8:28 "And we know that for those who love God all things work together for good, for those who are called according to his purpose."

I know, for me, it felt like a long road I was walking, more so on the days I couldn't walk, literally. For so many days, months, years I tried doing anything that would help me avoid pain, physical, emotional, and mental. Sometimes, it helped if I wasn't feeling guilty or felt the lazy look.

Because of so many things I wanted to do, but couldn't because my body would work long enough to make it worthwhile and enjoyable.

But even as I was trying to hide, little did I know God was using it for me to find Him, and draw me closer. As I said before in this book, and don't mind repeating, I never stopped to blame God. I already fell into the deepest well of despair. The only thing left was to grab the hand of Jesus to be lifted up.

I see others blaming God for their pain, and not making light of it, but the time to stop fighting Him is now. Situations, life circumstances, I'm sorry they happened, but they don't define who we are, or become us.

Sure they play a part in building our character, along with the evil done to us, or thrown against us. We can either keep blaming God, or stop fidgeting, and let Him apply rubbing alcohol, peroxide, whatever is needed to heal you, and make you whole again. The scars left will be signs of character maturity, proof of who God raised you to be.

Romans 8:28 "God is working all things together for your good to shine for His Glory. The 40 days in the wilderness may feel like 40 years, but we're never alone. Just like Moses wasn't alone, Jesus wasn't alone (and no, I'm not talking of satan) If we're truly saved by Jesus Christ as Savior then, the Holy Spirit is inside of us.

John 16:13 "When the Spirit of truth comes, he will guide you into all the truth, for he will not speak on his own authority, but whatever he hears he will speak, and he will declare to you the things that are to come." I know His Spirit was with me when I walked in the wilderness, and when I was writing poetry. Along the way, I discovered my own burning bushes, faced the devil's temptations, but it is written Jesus Christ is my victory. I've walked out victorious after being broken down, finally accepting God was up to something and let Him finish His good works.

In me, through me, His Work continues. I hope this book encourages you, inspires you to stop fighting God and let Him heal, guide you from being lost, hurt, and confused. I also hope my story gives you Humble Courage to share your story, even though you might struggle like me to believe the story is big and worthwhile enough to write.

Truth is, you never know who needs to hear your story to restore hope and to continue theirs. If you haven't already accepted Jesus into your heart to change you, heal you inside and out, let Him make you healthy by the foods of His spirit and of His Creation, the way He designed. I invite you to start your own Journey to Healing for a Life Restored of your own.

Salvation Prayer

Jesus I come before you confessing I am a sinner
Like it says in Romans I've fallen short I am guilty
The penalty of death should be mine, but it's yours

Jesus my spiritual eyes are now open to seeing Truth
Which is I am a sinner in need of being saved by you
I confess to believing you died on the cross to save me

Jesus come into my heart be Lord of my life and Save me
Resurrect me to come alive just like I believe You did for me
This Gospel I accept and is my Salvation Prayer, I am Yours

If you have read this, prayed this prayer, and believed in your heart
Welcome to the Kingdom of God, by Grace through Faith we're saved
In accepting Jesus as Savior we who were dead now live

3 Months Into Finding Answers

50 lbs. Lost

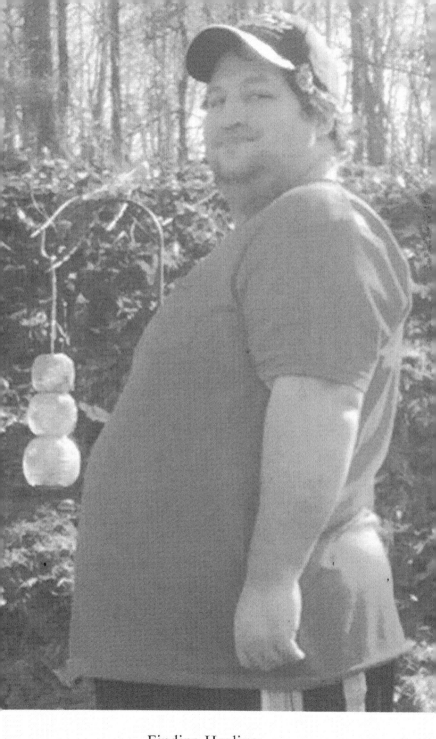

Finding Healing

Part Four

Favorite Things and Recipes

CHAPTER FORTY ONE
Favorite Things

BLUE FLOWER LOTUS tea, which I drank to deal with pain. I often put a bag in along with one of my other favorite teas.

Yogi teas, I pretty much love them all, but I used mostly what I felt my body was dealing with. Like Ginkgo Clarity to try and think clearer, green tea muscle recovery when dealing with a sore muscle after working out. It relaxed my mind to calm my thoughts before bed.

I still take pleasure in eating chocolate, but chocolate without sugar from a brand called Simply Lite and Lily's, but even though hard to do, don't eat too much. It will give you gas if digestion isn't use to the fiber. I try to have a little at the end of my meal, unless I made a cheesecake.

S. Pellegrino mineral water, especially with Italian lemon or lime juice, doesn't even need sweetener. But if you do:

Stevia without anything else added, especially Maltodextrin

Organic almond flour

Organic pasture raised chicken eggs, or range fed eggs
Grass fed beef when I could get it, if not still try and get
at least 80% 15g of fat, though really liked Kobe beef.

Oscar Mayer uncured bacon

Bob Evans all natural ground sausage

Farm Promise uncured ham and bacon

Seasonings like old bay, chili powder, turmeric, pink sea
salt

Dr. Berg products I recommend because they're real
ingredients and they work

And, of course, I recommend the Bible, getting to know
God and how He made every single detail of your body is a
must to know True healing.

CHAPTER FORTY TWO
Recipes

<u>Keto Stew</u>

1lb ground beef, 1 package of Bob Evans natural sausage cooked until browned. Remove grease, add cut up onions, and peppers, celery is good too, mixed in with the cooked meat. This is when I first start adding seasonings (old bay, chili powder). Then I add 1 can (big or small, up to you), depending on portion sizes. Make sure that every tomato can has no added sugars or sweeteners, 4g or less. I also add a can of tomato paste and sauce. I rinse out both cans halfway and dump them into pan. This is when I add 1/2 tablespoon of grass fed or pasture raised butter, also 3 tablespoons of unfortified nutritional yeast. I also sprinkle more seasoning. Now I start adding the veggies, peas, green beans, broccoli, brussels sprouts, kale, and, while cooking, sprinkle more seasonings. About 3 or 4 times during the whole cooking process, start to finish. By this time, if stove burner is set about 6, it should be close to boiling. Once it does boil and everything is added, turn it to simmer and stir time to time for about 45 to 50 minutes, or until veggies are tender. When done, I like adding shredded cheese on top. No crackers, otherwise it wouldn't be keto friendly. Enjoy.

By the way, sometimes I do add Spam from time-to-time (clean enough) experiment with your own choices.

*   *   *

<u>Almond Crust for Quiche Squares</u> (for pie just add 2 tsp of stevia, clean of hidden sweeteners)

1 and 2/3 to 2 cups Almond Flour (depending on pan size)

2/3 tsp baking powder, 1/2 tsp pink sea salt (Himalayan salt) "optional old bay seasoning, 2/3 tsp"

1/2 tsp vanilla, 1 large or 2 medium organic range fed eggs,

About 2/3 tbs grass fed butter melted. Mix together with

a fork.

Once mixed together, put in a greased with grass fed butter or gee

Preheat oven at 350 and bake crust for about 15 minutes

Quiche Recipe
3 to 5 eggs (depended medium or large eggs)
1 cup of almond milk unsweetened
1/2 cup organic heavy cream
2/3 tsp old bay
1/2 tsp pink salt

First, layer crust with ingredients. I do grass fed cheese first, then whatever ingredients you want.

My favorite is Bob Evans natural sausage and peas, but don't be afraid to experiment.

Then add egg mixture and bake at 350 for about 60 minutes, depending on thickness, or until you can stick through clean with fork.

*   *   *

<u>Cheesecake Squares</u>

Two 8 oz pasture raised cream cheese bars let soften

1/2 cup stevia (unless adding organic clean of hidden sweeteners chocolate) then can be less

2 eggs. Use beaters to mix btw cinnamon in crust is great too or in cheese part

You can mix in pumpkin or lemon juice (whichever you choose to make) as long as clean of too many added carbs. Once mixed, put in oven at 350 for 25 to 30 minutes, depending on size and thickness of pan. Then, once cooled, put it in the fridge or cold place to set for about 8 hours.

Never Alone

Acknowledgments

I would like to thank Jesus Christ my Savior for working through my weaknesses. I would like to thank my Parents for raising me right, and for being patient with me and for taking me to where I needed and wanted to go. I would like to thank my Uncles Tim and Steve for taking me golfing and giving me an outlet to give my mental side a break.

I would like to thank all of my cousins, and forgive me in not mentioning you by name. I would like to thank my Friends Jon, Daniel, Matthew, Josh and many more for giving me good characters to hangout with and to lean on. I would like to thank the Bug brothers under God Bible study group for good fellowship and giving me another place to get out of the house, to hear about Stepping up in Courage.

I would like to thank all the Pastors, Larry, Mike, Larry, John and youth Pastor Ron, Music Pastor Greg, Sunday school teachers, hearing God's message from you helped me grow in Faith and closer to Christ. I especially would like to thank Joshua Holmes, my book-making friend (who's a good author of 11 novels, please check his books out), without you my last 6 books wouldn't be possible, I'd still be searching for a purpose.

10577862R00114

Made in the USA
Lexington, KY
27 September 2018